THE NEW

Other books in this series:
AIDS and You by Patrick Dixon
Sex and You by Lance Pierson
The Occult and You by Roger Ellis

The New Age and You

ROGER ELLIS & ANDREA CLARKE

KINGSWAY PUBLICATIONS
EASTBOURNE

Unless otherwise indicated, biblical quotations are from the
New International Version © 1973, 1978, 1984 by
The International Bible Society.

Front cover design based on photo: The Image Bank

ISBN 0 86065 862 7

Printed in Great Britain for
KINGSWAY PUBLICATIONS LTD
Lottbridge Drove, Eastbourne, E Sussex BN23 6NT by
BPCC Hazells Ltd, Aylesbury, Bucks.
Typeset by J&L Composition Ltd, Filey, North Yorkshire

Contents

Contents

Foreword

Who can deny that science and technology have brought us massive advances over the last hundred years? The only problem has been the huge price of this great progress. For instance, we split the atom and created a frightening mass method of annihilating one another. We manufactured fertilisers and pesticides to produce more food for our growing population and polluted one of the earth's most precious resources – water. We developed advanced transport systems and the fuels to power them and left holes in the ozone layer. The same science that has brought us so many benefits has also threatened the very future of our planet.

But it's not just our science and technology that have let us down. The dream of materialism has turned out to be a nightmare. It's as though there is an enormous vacuum at the centre of our culture which we have been unable to fill with our possessions, or find answers to with even the best of technological advances. As we approach the year 2000, there is a growing feeling that we are at a critical point in human history when we must rethink our standards and values before it is too late. Many are reaching the conclusion that the reason for things being in such a mess is that we have lost touch with our spirituality. Enter the New Age!

In 1987, the *New Age Journal* conducted a survey in which it asked its readers for their definitions of the New Age. One reader summed it all up as 'a vision of a world transformed; a heaven on earth; a society in which the problems of today are overcome and a new existence emerges'. According to New Agers, our problems all stem from the fact that we have been living in the Age of Pisces. The major characteristics of this 'old age' are things which most of us would like to forget: war, injustice, inequality, hatred, mistrust, suffering and pain. The good news, according to the New Age movement, is that any time now the Age of Aquarius will dawn, which will bring with it peace and harmony, wholeness and fulfilment, as well as restoration for individuals, the world and the universe. Exactly when all this will happen depends to some extent on our attitudes, outlook and openness. So the New Ager's message is simple 'Get ready now by joining us. We are living just before the dawn of the new age of harmony and spiritual enlightenment, but quite how close the sunrise is, is down to us.'

The big question is, of course: does the New Age movement offer us genuine hope, or is it simply a rerun of the famous old story of the emperor's new clothes? The story where a smooth-talking salesman sells a rather gullible king a lie which not only costs him a fortune, but leaves him naked and looking very silly in more ways than one.

All this is why *The New Age and You* is an important book which I am glad to recommend. Not only is it very readable, but in it Roger Ellis and Andrea Clarke take a close look at the New Age movement's history and teaching and come up with an honest assessment of the reliability of its claims. If you are thinking about the message of the New Age, this book is for you.

Steve Chalke
The Oasis Trust
1992

1

Introducing the New Age

The TV guide flopped onto the door mat. In anticipation of the week ahead, Andrea ambled over to the front door to pick it up. Cuddly Russell Grant grinned cheekily from the front page wearing an 'easy to knit sun sign sweater, see page 92'. Being a self-confessed telly addict, she settled herself down on the sofa to plan her week's viewing. She never knew there was so much in it!

It must be a very difficult task to provide a menu of programmes to cater for all tastes. If we were in charge of a TV station, the week's viewing would take on a whole new look. In Andrea's opinion all sport would be banned. No more endlessly boring cricket matches. Gone would be Saturday afternoon football, and instead she would schedule the kind of comedy films that she spends a fortune hiring from the video shop.

Flicking through the pages of the TV guide, it was easy to see that a lot of thought had gone into the coming week's programme plan. Something for all the family. A new series entitled *The New Age* was starting on Sunday evening. There was a health and fitness programme that promised an in-depth look at alternative health techniques for the mind and body.

An arts programme was examining the world of psychedelia, while *QED* was to investigate the use of crystals and pyramids. On Tuesday Arthur C. Clarke would be looking at newly reported sightings of UFOs and *The Business Programme* would show how meditation and hypnosis are proving successful in relieving executive stress and increasing productivity. Wogan would be interviewing New Age guru Shirley MacLaine about her revelatory experiences with various channelled entities, and of course dear old Russell Grant would be there to brighten up the day providing astrological advice all wrapped up in a lovely fluffy 'easy to knit sun sign sweater, see page 92'.

What is this thing called the New Age? Magazines are full of it, the television feeds us a constant diet of the ideas and techniques of the rich and famous who claim to be 'New Agers', and all of us—young and old—are slowly but surely being conditioned to accept that this really is 'the dawning of the age of Aquarius'.

Whether you realise it yet or not, unless you have been wrapped in several layers of thick cotton wool for most of your life you have already been affected by this thing called the New Age. This influence seems destined to increase. The New Age has arrived with a vengeance, and, like us, you only have to read the TV guide to see that its influence has begun to spread through education, medicine, business and finance, science, religion, sport and good old family entertainment.

Since you have decided to read this book, we can fairly safely assume that the New Age intrigues you. Whatever your interest, whether you know nothing about it or indeed, even if you are actively involved in the New Age, you will want to know the answers to questions like: 'What is this thing called the New Age?', 'Where has it come from?', 'Who's in charge of it?' and, 'Should I be involved in it?' Well, rest assured that this book has been written, not to blind you with science, but to answer the basic questions about the New Age. Armed with the facts, you can then decide what your response to this growing phenomenon will be.

In researching this subject, however, we have discovered that it is almost impossible to sum up the New Age in a few short sentences. Even New Agers don't seem to agree 100% on what it actually is. Roger, who is a keen fisherman, likens it to trying to catch hold of a very slippery 25lb carp without a landing net. Just when you think you've got a handle on it, it changes direction slightly and slips out of your hands. However, a fish is a fish whichever way you look at it, and the New Age, although a bit of a slippery character, does have several basic characteristics. It is these characteristics that we seek to 'put the net round' by outlining them for you in the following chapters.

Countdown to the New Age

No one can deny that life in the final decade of the twentieth century is not easy. So much is uncertain. On the personal front we are faced with the prospect that at least one in three marriages are likely to end in divorce, and that more children will be born into one-parent families than in any other century. The cost of living is rising even as we write, and while a war is always raging somewhere, a major recession affects us all. Globally we are now having to confront the issue of the damage that has been caused through our neglect of the planet's environment. Meanwhile, daily adverts warn us not to 'die of ignorance', as the virulent HIV virus threatens lives at every level. The age of materialism is breathing its last as more and more people are waking up to the fact that the fast food, buy now, pay later attitude to life is taking its toll.

According to New Age astrologer Virginia Kay Miller,

> The world is in the midst of a massive upheaval . . . Many people believe that humankind is on the verge of an evolutionary breakthrough and we are standing on the threshold of a New Age. Called the 'Aquarian Age', it will bring about a new world order in which individuals will realise their spiritual being and their interconnectedness with all life. To survive . . . as a planet, we must develop the Aquarian consciousness, which recognises that we are all linked together as members of the human race and as inhabitants of planet Earth.[1]

(By the way, don't panic if some of the language that New Agers use seems like gobbledygook. You will find that we have included an A–Z of the New Age to help you speak the lingo!—See Chapter 2.)

One of the central themes of the New Age is this: we are on the verge of an incredible evolutionary quantum leap. Man has throughout history undergone several transitionary periods, moving slowly but surely towards the ultimate goal of civilisation, thought to be self-realisation. We have come on in leaps and bounds from the days of the cavemen, due to the revolutions that have taken place in our thinking. Once, we thought the earth was flat and all travellers feared that if they went too far they would fall off the edge, but now, since the earth has been circumnavigated, we realise that this is not true and our perception of the globe has been altered dramatically.

The agricultural revolution made it possible for the average man to think beyond simply producing enough food for his own family, and so his horizons were widened. The later industrial revolution paved the way for a massive growth in the population and so began the rise of the industrial, technologically minded society that we find ourselves in today.

Throughout the ages there have been significant times of great social upheaval that have come about as man has sought to discover and uncover the mysteries of life itself. People have been expected to grasp new concepts which radically alter their thinking and inevitably affect their actions. Once it was thought impossible for man to fly; now, while we sit on a British Airways 747 winging its way to an exotic holiday destination, we can sip Bacardi and Coke and read about the latest exploits of the US shuttle crew installing satellites that will beam signals all around the world.

Based upon the predictions of astrological time scales, New Agers are preparing for a leap out of the age of Pisces, which is characterised by a need to conform to physical and material patterns, and straight into the age of Aquarius, a time where they are certain that there will be widespread peace and prosperity as people become aware of spiritual things. This does sound like very good news at the moment. After all, who would want to pass up the chance to be part of a society offering such great perks? New

Agers are so sold on the idea of a changed society that they are keen to sell the concept at all levels, which is why the New Age is being marketed so successfully into every sphere of influence. If you really believe in the product, then you will be convincing and people will be impressed enough to buy. In the words of Victor Kiam, of Remington Microscreen fame, 'I was so impressed I bought the company.'

So what's the catch? In order to facilitate the coming of the New Age that has been threatening to dawn since the sixties, we need to change. And that's the catch. In later chapters we will be exploring just exactly what changes we are being asked to make in order to mould ourselves into an acceptable shape for the New Age. All of us recognise the need for progress, and looking at the current world scene who could deny that some serious thinking and solution seeking are needed? But let's not be hasty. If New Agers are telling us that we are on the verge of a change in which the new Man 'will be as superior to present day humanity as we are to the apes', we need to be certain that we are embracing the truth and are not in pursuit of a myth.

So what's new?

Where does the New Age come from? The Bible tells us that there is nothing new under the sun, and the New Age is no exception. As we begin to look at it more closely we will see that, in fact, the only thing that is relatively new about the New Age is the way that it is being marketed in today's western culture.

But it must have started somewhere. Let's take a

quick look at the more modern origins of what is in essence one of the oldest tricks in the book.

C. S. Lewis said of world religions, 'Hinduism and Christianity alone offer the only viable options, because Hinduism absorbs all religious systems, and Christianity excludes all others, maintaining the supremacy of the claims of Jesus Christ.'[2]

In the nineteenth century, many western philosophers began to look into the wisdom of the east. Drawing from ancient Hindu scriptures such as the *Bhagavad Gita*, they explored the possibilities of controlling the mind using the meditational techniques used for centuries by Hindus in their search for spiritual enlightenment. Their experiences with transcendentalism would later bring about the popular growth of the Transcendental movement.

'You're feeling very sleepy'

An Austrian physician called Franz Mesmer (1734–1814) began to teach 'mesmeric sleep' techniques to willing Americans. Introducing it as a new method of mental healing, he and his disciples, including Mary Baker Patterson Eddy, taught that disease was caused by false beliefs and not physical disorders. Out of this came Christian Science, Divine Science, Science of Mind, Religious Science and the Unity School of Christianity. In altering the conscious state through hypnotic trances, it was discovered that individuals were able to do things and know things that they would otherwise be incapable of, and so the door opened to spiritualism.

'Is anybody there?'

There was an explosive interest in exploring the unknown world after two sisters claimed to be able to contact the spirit of a murdered pedlar whose body lay under the basement of their home. They would receive messages as the spirit allegedly knocked out a code for them to interpret. Though it was later discovered that the Fox sisters had in fact been hoaxing this phenomenon (one of the sisters confessed to having caused the noises by cracking her knee joints!), hundreds of people began to join in the craze to contact spirits 'beyond the grave'.

The Theosophical Society is acknowledged by many to be one of the major influences in founding what we know to be the modern New Age movement. Madame Helena Petrovna Blavatsky (1831–91) was an eccentric Russian mystic who claimed to have received revelation regarding world affairs from the 'ascended masters'—a group of people who had evolved to a higher spiritual plane. While the general public were busy sitting in darkened rooms attempting to contact their dearly departed uncle Charlie, Madame Blavatsky (who incidentally lived a life full of unbelievable scandal, eventually dying amid accusations that she was a fraud) was returning from India to unleash a 'westernised' Hinduism and occult formula that would be the grounding of the remarkably successful Theosophical Society, founded in 1875.

She and her followers—Annie Besant (1847–1933), Guy Ballard (1878–1939) and Alice Bailey (1880–1949)—actively promoted spiritism, seances and basic Hindu philosophy. Boasting of her great ability to sway masses to accept her teachings, Blavatsky declared, 'In every part of the world people have turned into asses at my whistle and have obediently wagged their long ears as I piped my tune.'[3]

Alice Bailey was perhaps one of the most significant influences of the time, and it was she who was the first to coin the term 'New Age'. She wrote more than twenty books under the influence of spirits (not of the alcoholic kind) who allegedly guided her telepathically to understand that a time was coming when a new master would come to show erring mankind the error of our ways. This ultimate messianic figure, known as the Lord Maitreya, was billed to be the final incarnation of all the 'enlightened ones' who had preceded him. Unfortunately, Alice Bailey's spirit guides must have had their wires crossed since some of her 'prophetic' writings have not only proved to be inaccurate, but are, on close examination, contradictory. The Theosophical Society certainly fuelled the emerging New Age movement, even though it suffered personally, when it planned for the Lord Maitreya to appear in the person of one of Annie Besant's proteges, Krishna Murti. He unfortunately declined the honour of this great anointing because his brother died, and he had in his grief-stricken state become rather disillusioned with the claims of the society (not quite the 'ascended master' they had expected).

It has to be said that not all New Agers hold to the idea of a 'messianic' figure emerging, but for some the search still continues. As a point of interest, Robert Kennedy (the president's brother) was assassinated by Sirhan Sirhan, from the Middle East, who was a vehement follower of the teachings of the Theosophical Society. Other famous adherents have been: George

Bernard Shaw, Thomas Eddison, William Butler Yeats and Yawaharlal Nehru.

While the term 'New Age' was being used at the turn of the century, it was not until the sixties that 'the age of Aquarius' was popularised after the title song of the musical *Hair*. Many westerners went off to the east to find wisdom for themselves on the trail of the ancient mystics, while the eastern mystics were hot-footing it to the west. Spiritual masters, gurus and swamis arrived en masse to promote their philosophies and techniques in easy-to-swallow westernised chunks. Among them were Indian Swami Vivekananda, who formed the Vedanta Society; Paramahansa Yogananda, who established the Self-Realisation fellowship; the infamous and later deported mystical teacher, Bhagwan Shree Rajneesh; and Meher Baba (these are all real names) who founded the Islamic-oriented Friends of Meher Baba group.

There had been stirrings in the contemporary medicine camp for some time as the writings of the famous psychoanalysts Sigmund Freud and Carl Jung were challenging the established foundational theories surrounding human behaviour. And on the scientific front, the world was being turned upside-down as the consequences of Albert Einstein's $E=MC^2$ theory were unleashed upon the unwitting populations of Hiroshima and Nagasaki. But to most of us, the New Age can be most profoundly attributed to the hippies.

Tune in and drop out

Born in the sixties, while we grappled with our nappies we unfortunately missed the delights of the psychedelic decade summed up in images of brightly coloured outrageous clothes, bangles, beads, the smell of incense and marijuana, rock concerts and political demos. The history books tell us that after the Second World War the teenager emerged, a product of marketing moguls who realised that there was an untapped source of revenue in this age group who for the first time in years had some money to spend. A youth culture emerged, sold on the idea that they could buy out of the outmoded world of their parents by buying into a new kind of fashion and individual 'youth identity' closely related to the new style of music that was taking off in underground clubs. The teenagers of the fifties were 'wild' by past standards, but, like the tragic James Dean, they were in the most part 'rebels without a cause'. That was until the sixties.

Already disillusioned by the materialistic, moral treadmill that was associated so strongly with the westernised culture of the day, individuals began to search for an escape route. The spiritual imagination of the western world had for too long been crushed by the work ethic that said that hard work, restraint and discipline were to be embraced at all costs, and so, out of this sterile, 'square' environment, the sixties counter-culture was born.

The Vietnam War, problems with racial inequality and a failing economy drove thousands of students to challenge 'the system' at all levels. There was a rising interest in the political ideology of the 'new left' neo-Marxists, as more and more people were encouraged to look beyond traditional values to discover new horizons of experience.

It was in the mid-sixties that Hinduism really began to make its mark in the west, when the infamous

Maharishi Mahesh Yogi took popular heroes The Beatles under his wing. Teaching Transcendental Meditation (TM) and all manner of eastern metaphysics wrapped up as western psychology and science, he was instrumental in leading many to adopt eastern mysticism as the framework for their life and thinking. Many became involved in the sects and cults that sprang up at this time, convinced of the benefit of discovering and developing this previously untapped spirituality and assured that they were truly on the road to real freedom in the hands of an assortment of largely self-professed swamis, gurus, yogis and 'enlightened ones'. Sadly, many never found freedom. They emerged as casualties who'd been ripped off, manipulated and disillusioned. For them, the path back to normality was slow and painful.

For others, though, it was a time to 'let it all hang out', using phrases like 'if it feels good, do it' and 'do your own thing'. Experimentation in all things was encouraged, and hallucinogenic drugs and a revival in the occult opened the doors to experiences that were to say the least 'far out!' from the norm. The road to the east became a well-worn path as many decided to make pilgrimages in search of spiritual fulfilment. To 'drop out' of society was a popular career option of the time.

Seventies flairs and lots of hair

The sixties passed by. The Beatles split up, and though George Harrison and John Lennon still championed the causes of those heady 'flower power' days, the scene began to change. Hippies were radical and Utopian in their ideas. The young people who had left the west in search of eastern promise began to return to a post-hippie culture in which the 'human potential movement' was captivating the imagination of the public.

'We use only 10% of our human potential. We can tap into the dormant 90%.' The seventies were marked by the spoon-bending antics of Uri Geller who claimed that he had developed the human abilities of ESP and 'mind over matter'. Andrea vividly remembers sitting in front of the television screen, when about six years old, holding on to a broken hair-dryer as Uri Geller claimed to be projecting his 'mental abilities' across the airwaves in order to 'zap' electrical objects back into operation. The hair-dryer remained irreparable and was later thrown away. However, several people phoned in to the programme claiming that their fridges, washing machines and long dead toasters had been miraculously resurrected.

Anything 'weird' was OK as long as it wasn't seen to be associated with 'religion'. There was a growing suspicion of the once popular cults and sects. This was no doubt heightened by the news of the Jonestown 'mass suicide' in which Jim Jones, leader of a commune of 915 people in the Guyanan jungle, convinced his followers, including members of his own family, to take cyanide capsules in a ceremony that would mark their leaving behind this outmoded world and facilitating their triumphant entry into the next.

Sell, sell, sell!

While the sixties were radical and extreme, and the seventies saw an increase of spiritual awareness from a more balanced position, the eighties emerged as the decade in which the 'New Age' would firmly establish itself, not as a counter-culture but as part of the acceptable mainstream.

The eighties generation was characterised by a need to improve. Materialism was at its peak, and a survey of school leavers revealed that the highest priority of their time was money. Yuppies, with their high tech, executive lifestyles, clothed in designer labels and clutching their filofaxes, were sold on the pursuit of excellence. 'Have it all! Be somebody!' was the commercial message. Chasing after the dream, a new social crisis was identified: stress.

Escaping from the detrimental symptoms of hectic, stressful lives became an increasingly popular priority, and the marketing corporations, always keen to jump on the bandwagon of changing social trends in order to make a fast buck, began to promote products and techniques that would help. Alternatives to traditional medicine were sought out, and the market expanded as more and more people realised that prescribed pills and potions were just not hitting the spot. There was a move to get back to nature, but this time the emphasis was less on getting out of the rat race, but more on incorporating nature back into it. Products proudly proclaimed that they had no additives or preservatives, and the sale of vitamin supplements soared.

It was in the early eighties that Marilyn Ferguson wrote her bestselling book, *The Aquarian Conspiracy*. Hailed as the unofficial New Age Bible, it outlined the vision and the agenda for personal and social transformation and encouraged all to reach out for the future, exploring their potential towards the Aquarian age of 'the mind's true liberation'.[4]

Actress Shirley MacLaine became the high priestess

of the New Age as her books, and then her television series, *Out on a Limb*, charted her reluctant voyage of discovery into the spiritual realm that included meditation, trance channelling, past life recall, out-of-body experiences, conversations with extra-terrestrials, and much more, alongside tabloid revelations of her steamy love life with, among others, an unnamed politician. 'I'm just a human being trying to find some answers about what we are doing here, where we came from and where we are going.'[5] Her message was proclaimed to TV and newspaper interviewers alike, appealing to the general public who, remembering her Oscar-winning performances, enrolled in their thousands to take part in her two-day seminars called 'Connecting with the Higher Self'.

Behind the scenes, David Spangler, a key figure in the early development of the model New Age community of Findhorn on the eastern coast of Scotland, continued to promote the work of Alice Bailey through the Lucifer Trust, later renamed the Lucis Trust. The trust is a kind of occult forum (highly influenced by the writings of Alice Bailey), and though it claims to have no formal doctrine or creed, it is basically centred around the New Age concepts of acquiring expanded consciousness, communion with supernatural beings and an eastern philosophy of life and death.

The Findhorn community gained public notoriety with its successful production of hugely oversized vegetables, claiming that these were a sign from nature of the truth that was established there. (The vegetables are now down to their normal size, so their methods are not about to solve the world food problem.)

On 16th and 17th August, 1987, 144,000 people

were to gather at 350 'sacred sites' around the globe 'to synchronise the earth with the rest of the galaxy'. Known as the Harmonic Convergence, it was billed as the 'cosmic trigger' that would usher in world peace and harmony. In reality, only 20,000 turned up to tune in, and the massive UFO sightings and the 'great, unprecedented outpourings of extra-terrestrial intelligence' promised by its founder Jose Arguelles never materialised.

Into the nineties

American opinion polls have observed that 42% of Americans have sought to contact the dead, thirty million (one in four) believe in reincarnation, 14% endorse spiritist mediums (trance channellers) and 67% of adults read astrology, 37% of whom believe that it is actually scientific. Despite its eastern roots and occultic links, the New Age has begun to infiltrate society at all levels. And not just in the USA, but increasingly so in Britain.

Flicking through the TV guide, it becomes clear that the media have begun to pick up on this thing called the New Age like never before, and the imagination of the general public is being captured as we head fast and furiously towards a new millennium.

The New Age movement is eclectic; it draws from many sources. It appeals because it allows individuals, as never before, to do what they feel is right for them, with no rigid constraints. There is no one way for the New Ager. All roads lead the same way, to self-realisation; all roads, that is, except for the one that claims to exclude all others: orthodox Christianity.

Like never before there is a cry from all levels of

society to get it right this time. There is a race on to save the globe from environmental disaster. The current world scene is not a settled one, and the search for the truth has increased. It is becoming increasingly fashionable to discuss what we believe, and to accept that a spiritual realm has taken precedence over the atheistic 'there is nothing' approach to reality.

At a recent Green Consumer Exhibition, the entrance fee also included free admission to its partner conference, The Festival of Body, Mind and Spirit, with its choice of seminars including: occultic healing, astrology, crystal power, energy mastery, past-life therapy, the psychic world, Krishna consciousness, and mythology and relationships. Sadly, for many, 'going green' will unwittingly also involve a subtle and gradual conversion to New Age spirituality, as the important environmental issues have been grasped with enthusiasm by New Agers.

From this potted history of the New Age, we can see that it is only now in the nineties that it is really coming of age. The stage is being set for more and more people to be influenced by philosophies that we have seen are not really new at all. The New Age is in essence not really a movement, if by that we mean that it has a distinct and tangible headquarters. Nor can it be treated as a cult, as there is no one leader, although there are those who are very vocal about their allegiance to the New Age. As we explore further the basic philosophies of the New Age, we will see how it has been shaped by ancient occultism and has links into the philosophies of the ancient Egyptians, American Indians, Babylonians, Persians, Paganism, Hinduism, Buddhism, Taoism and several other 'isms'.

Putting the world back together

A teacher gave a child a map of the world that she had found in a magazine and ripped it into small pieces. She handed it to one of the children in her class and asked him to go away and piece 'the world' back together again. She was confident that this would be an impossible task. The following day the child marched up to her desk and handed her the map of the world, perfectly pieced together. Amazed, she asked him how he had managed to do the impossible. 'Easy,' he replied, and turning the map over he showed her that on the other side there was a picture of a man. 'I knew that to put the world together was too difficult, so I concentrated on putting the man together and then the whole thing came back into one piece.'

New Agers use this story to illustrate the need for individuals to concentrate on personal transformation through 'enlightening' mind consciousness-changing techniques so that the world can become 'one' again.

Christians, coming from a different angle, also see that the answer lies in a man. The Bible tells us that it is only through Jesus Christ that we can experience true 'wholeness' as we accept that God's only Son really is 'the way and the truth and the life' (Jn 14:6). He is the man on whom future change can be centred.

2

Parlez-Vous New Age?

Have you ever tried to have a conversation with someone who insists on using jargon and clichés in every sentence? It can be infuriating, especially when you haven't got the faintest idea what the person is going on about. You valiantly try to keep up, but in reality they might just as well be speaking in a foreign language.

Very often you find an index of peculiar words and phrases on the final pages of a book. The trouble is, you often don't discover it until you've struggled your way from front to back. We have identified that it is increasingly likely that all of us will have some form of contact with the New Age in the not-so-distant future, if not already. It is important, therefore, that we become familiar with some of the words and phrases commonly used by New Agers—then we can successfully speak the lingo!

This A–Z is not exhaustive, and not all New Agers adhere to everything included in this directory. It's probably best not to read it all at once, but rather to use it as a resource to dip in and out of.

Acupuncture/acupressure

A holistic health technique from Ancient Chinese medicine and philosophy. Disease is thought to be caused by an imbalance in the flow of 'life energy' in the body; by inserting either needles or pressure to key points on the body this flow is supposedly redirected and a healing established.

Agent

A person sending a telepathic message.

Age of Aquarius

Astrologers believe that evolution goes through cycles of 2,000–2,400 years which correspond with the signs of the zodiac. New Agers believe that we are about to move from the Age of Pisces to the Age of Aquarius. This age will supposedly be a time where people are more aware of spiritual things and will be in tune with the cosmos.

Akashic records (also known as Universal mind or Memory of nature)

A vast cosmic record of knowledge of every thought, word or deed of every person who has ever lived. It is supposed to be impossible to destroy or corrupt and is said to be located in a region of space known as 'the ether'.

Alchemy

Medieval folklore holds that it is possible to turn base metals to gold. This is often used as an illustration of the change or transformation of base human nature to the divine that New Agers say will occur as we enter the Age of Aquarius.

Alpha

The physical body.

Altered states

States other than normal waking consciousness, eg day-dreaming, sleep dreaming, hypnotic trance, meditative, mystical or drug-induced states, and unconsciousness.

Amulets/Lucky charms

Objects worn superstitiously and carried as symbols of protection. These objects are sometimes used because they are assumed to have healing properties in themselves, eg copper for arthritis. Some charms are in the form of occult symbols or an idol. They could be inscribed or have a spell cast on them.

Animism

The belief that inanimate things (such as plants) possess a soul or spirit. The rise of belief in Mother Earth and the increasing popularity of Stonehenge and Glastonbury have seen many people turning to animism, nature religion and paganism, believing that they are rededicating the earth.

Anthroposophy

A system of thought founded by German mystic Rudolf Steiner. Anthroposophy means 'wisdom of man' and it teaches that we possess the truth within us.

Ascended masters

Supposedly, these are individuals who have been 'highly evolved' and no longer need to undergo lives in the physical plane in order to achieve spiritual growth. They are said to be guides to help in the spiritual evolution of mankind. These masters are believed to be contacted by spiritist-type activity.

Ascension of Christ (the New Age version)

This is reinterpreted in a mystical way to refer to the rise of the Christ Consciousness in mankind, a rising awareness that man is divine.

Astral/Astral plane

The non-physical level of existence characterised by emotion. This is said to be the place where most humans go after they die and where they exist between earthly lives.

Astral body

The spiritual, non-material body supposedly possessed by all humans (and in some beliefs all living things) which continues to exist (or separates) after bodily death.

Astral projection/Flight or travel

The temporary experience of leaving one's body, which is particularly dangerous. This is achieved by some through meditation techniques, and by others through taking hallucinogenic drugs like LSD or so-called magic mushrooms. Others have experienced this alleged phenomenon during yoga exercises or even on the operating table.

Astrology

The art or pseudo-science of interpreting the influence that cosmic forces radiating from 'celestial bodies' supposedly have on any part of the universe, particularly humans. It originated around 5,000 years ago, probably in Babylon. It is based on the belief that the earth is the centre of the universe, circled by the zodiac, and it is used to predict future events, analyse people's characters and plan people's lives, based on the time, place and date of their birth.

Attunement/At-one-ment

A technique that relates to the New Age idea that complete oneness with God, who is said to be in all things including each individual, can be attained through various methods such as meditation.

Aura

A force field or energy field around the body or inanimate objects which is normally visible (according to those who believe in it). Its colour or colours are said to indicate different aspects of the subject's physical, psychological and spiritual condition.

Automatic writing

Writing that is produced without the conscious thought of the person using the pen or typewriter. Often associated with séances or channelling.

Avatar

A person who descends from the highest evolutionary plane to take on human form as a manifestation of divinity, revealing divine truth to people. An avatar has no need to be reincarnated into another body because there is no bad **karma** to work off.

Bhagavad Gita

A Sanskrit poem which relates a conversation between Krishna and Arjuna. It is part of Krishna's revelation, called an Upanishad, and is held as a sacred scripture by Hindus.

Biofeedback

A technique to self-monitor normally unconscious, involuntary processes such as brainwaves, heartbeat and muscle tension, and then to try to consciously control internal biological functions.

Blood of Christ (the New Age version)

Understood by some New Agers to refer to the 'life energy of the Cosmic Christ'. This blood supposedly flowed from the cross into the etheric (or spiritual) realms of the earth. From these realms the Christ seeks to guide the spiritual evolution of mankind.

Bodhisattva

A being said to have earned the right to enter Nirvana, having achieved complete enlightenment, but who has chosen instead to turn back and help humanity to attain that same goal. The Christ is said to be a Bodhisattva.

Buddha

The 'enlightened one', an avatar or messenger, supremely Gautama Siddhartha, born in 563 BC, who taught an eightfold path to spiritual enlightenment or Nirvana.

Centring

A technique based on the idea that energy flows throughout the body and that 'well-being' can be attained by balancing the flow of energy and 'attuning' with the energy, or centring yourself to it.

Chakras

According to New Agers and yogis these are seven energy points on the human body.

Channelling

A New Age form of mediumship or spiritism, where the channeller is controlled by a spirit entity who will impart paranormal information.

Charms

Words that have **magical** powers.

Clairaudience

Ability to hear without using the ears, the voice or voices of spirit guides or channelled entities.

Clairvoyance

Ability to see things beyond the ordinary and beyond this time scale without using the eyes. Also called **Second Sight**.

Consciousness

Mental awareness of present reality. New Agers call for a consciousness revolution in which individuals will be aware of their inner divinity and will as a result look at life in a totally new way, understanding the 'oneness' of all things.

Control

The spirit that controls a **medium** while in a trance.

Cosmic Christ

The Christ is said to be a universal spirit or cosmic force whose goal is to guide the spiritual evolution of mankind.

Cosmic consciousness

A spiritual and mystical awareness that 'all is one'. To attain cosmic consciousness is to see the universe as God and God as the universe (**pantheism**).

Cosmic humanism

Mankind is the ultimate. There is unlimited potential in every human being because of his or her inner divinity.

Crystals

New Agers believe crystals contain incredible healing and energising powers and are supposedly able to restore the body's 'energy flow'. Crystals are often used as tools to promote out-of-body experiences and enhance meditation, and it is often said that you do not choose your crystal but rather your crystal chooses you.

Cult

A religious organisation based on and built around the teachings of a central character whose authority is held equal to or greater than the established scriptures of the major religions.

Déjà-vu

The feeling that a new place or event has somehow been experienced before. This often leads to the assumption of past lives.

Dharma

Law, truth or teaching; used to express the central teachings of Hindu and Buddhist religion. Dharma implies that essential truth can be stated about the way things are and that people should comply with that truth.

Direct voice

While in a trance, a medium's voice is taken over by a control spirit or another spirit. Sometimes the accent or tone is totally different from that of the medium.

Discarnate

The soul or personality of a living creature who has died (and is separated from the physical body).

Divination

A broad category which includes various means of attaining knowledge not available naturally. This knowledge is obtained by occult techniques which produce results that can be interpreted. For example, horoscopes, consulting the dead, reading cards, reading natural phenomena.

Dowsing

Using a forked rod or stick of hazel wood, this is a method to 'divine' the whereabouts of underground or hidden water, oil, buried money, lost articles or even people, alive or dead.

Earth Logos

The Earth Logos is supposedly the spiritual being who is the ensouling life of planet earth. The earth is considered to be the physical manifestation of this spiritual intelligence.

Ectoplasm

Occultists claim that there is a mysterious fluid-like white substance that comes from a medium's body while contacting a spirit.

Esalen Institute

A growth centre located in California which offers mind, body, spirit workshops and seminars.

Esoteric

Any knowledge that is known only to a few.

ESP (extra-sensory perception)

Formerly known as the sixth sense, this is an experience of, a response to, or a knowledge of an event or object that could not have been gained through our normal senses. It relates to divination, clairvoyance and telepathy.

EST (Erhard Seminars Training)

Another New Age training centre that provides workshops specifically designed for professional and business people.

Evocation/Invocation

Evocation is the calling forth of a dangerous evil spirit by means of spoken or written words. Often an area is ritually marked out in which the evoked spirit is supposed to stay. Invocation is the calling up of a so-called good spirit by similar means. Both these processes are potentially very dangerous.

Fall of man (New Age version)

This is a phrase New Agers use to describe the fall of man's consciousness to a state that only recognises the existence of the material realm. The Christ is believed to have 'redeemed' man by helping to reveal the spiritual world. (See also **Gnosticism**.)

Findhorn Community

A world-famous New Age community in northern Scotland that offers education, training and a 'whole lifestyle' package based on the principles of New Age spirituality.

Firewalking

A spiritistic ceremony to show the human ability (under the influence of spirits) to walk over a bed of very hot coals with no physical harm. This is often faked, but by no means always.

Fortune-telling

Foretelling of the future (predictive divination).

Freud

Sigmund Freud, the famous psychoanalyst who practised hypnotherapy and popularised ideas such as dream interpretation therapy, linking human behaviour to the sexual impulse.

Gaia

A Greek name for the goddess of the earth worshipped in paganism. This also refers to James Lovelock's pseudo-scientific hypothesis that all living matter on earth is really one single living organism, and humanity is the 'nervous system' of the living earth.

Globalism

Many New Agers believe that the world must no longer be divided by individual nations and many states but should become one, a one-world community demonstrating the oneness of all things.

Gnosticism

The ancient belief or tradition which holds that salvation comes through the realisation that man is divine and of the same essence in every way as God. This knowledge is secret or hidden, and when discovered by the individual is claimed to free one from the 'illusion' of the material world.

God

New Agers talk about God as a being with 'many faces'. He, She or It (there is differing opinion) is referred to as Universal Consciousness, or Universal Life, or Universal Energy. The New Age God is more or less an impersonal 'force' that 'is'.

Great Invocation

A New Age prayer translated into eighty languages, used to invoke the presence of the Cosmic Christ on earth and lead to the oneness and brotherhood of all mankind.

Group guru

A slang term used to describe the New Age idea that the Cosmic Christ is in all people and therefore mankind is a single guru. (In simple English, we are all supposed to know everything, we just don't know it yet.)

Guru

Teacher or master specifically of spiritual things, whose goal is to instruct and lead disciples to enlightenment. A guru's authority is to be accepted without question.

Harmonic convergence

Assembly of New Age meditators gathered at a particular astrological time in strategic locations (energy points) to usher in peace on earth, one-world government and the Age of Aquarius.

Higher self/Inner self

The part of one's self that is supposedly the most spiritual and knowing. New Agers claim this 'higher self' can be channelled for wisdom and guidance. Also known as the Superconsciousness, the Atman, the Oversoul, the Christ (or Krishna or Buddha) Consciousness, or simply as the God within.

Holism

The theory that all things are one whole, interrelated and interdependent.

Holistic health

Sees the body as interrelated and therefore aims to treat the 'whole person'—body, mind, spirit—and not just a separate illness or disease.

Humanism

A philosophical system where human beings are rated above any God or spirituality. Man is held as the measure for all things.

Human potential movement

A movement based in humanism, where man's essential goodness and unlimited potential are stressed.

Hypnosis

In a state similar to deep sleep, or a trance, the hypnotised person acts according to the suggestions of the hypnotist. Used by New Agers as an aid to uncovering subconscious knowledge of the supernatural/spiritual realm.

I Ching

A Chinese book of divination associated with Taoism. A system of fortune-telling where sticks are thrown into six-sided figures.

Initiation

Used when referring to a person's consciousness in the process of expansion or transformation. There are levels or degrees of initiation as the initiate becomes aware of inner realities.

Interconnectedness/Interdependence

Terms used by New Agers when referring to the concept that everything in the universe is one and therefore completely linked.

Intuition

Ability to have knowledge beyond conscious or ordinary reasoning.

Jesus (of the New Age)

An avatar who gained attunement to the Cosmic Christ Consciousness and was able to be a manifestation of the divine for three years in order to teach all people that they themselves are God.

Kabalah (or Qabbalah or Cabala)

Jewish occult mysticism developed by certain rabbis, especially during the Middle Ages. It relies on mathematical interpretation of the Bible and involves various forms of fortune-telling, magic, altered states of consciousness, and spiritism.

Karma

A Hindu word which refers to the law of cause and effect. Supposedly a debt is accumulated by each soul as a result of positive and negative deeds in a life or many lives and this then determines the outcome of the soul's next life.

Kirlian photography

A high-frequency electrical process which produces a photo-like image of an apparent electrical field that allegedly surrounds living beings. It is considered to be a means of photographing the **aura** and diagnosing illness and depression.

Kundalini

Psycho-spiritual energy or the 'elemental' energy which is claimed to lie coiled like a snake at the base of the spine. The aim of Kundalini yoga is to release this energy, awakening the snake and bringing spiritual awareness and enlightenment.

Levitation

The lifting of a person or object from the ground not by physical means but by the exertion of psychic powers.

Ley lines

Straight geological lines of spiritual force that some adherents of pagan religions believe were discovered and used in the Neolithic period. Their existence is said to be demonstrated by the many alignments between religious sites. There is no archeological support for this view, though many ancient religious sites do seem to be aligned with one another.

Glastonbury and Stonehenge are key sites where ley lines are said to converge.

Lucis Trust

Originally the Lucifer Publishing Company, the Trust now publishes New Age books worldwide and owns all copyrights to the Alice Bailey books.

Magic (black and white)

Exercising power over or attempting to manipulate evil spirits. The idea is to subvert, manipulate or dominate people or situations for your own ends by spirit power. Black magic is supposed to be for selfish or destructive purposes and white magic for 'benevolent' purposes. In reality, both black and white magic are evil and dangerous and lie at the bottom of the occult.

Magic mushrooms

Mushrooms with hallucinogenic properties that are found growing wild. They are eaten to induce out-of-body experiences.

Maitreya

The name has been linked to an ancient Buddha, but some New Agers believe that in 1977 there was the second coming of Christ in the person of the Maitreya.

Mandala

A design which is supposed to enable one to concentrate and focus all one's attention to a single point.

Mantra

A word or phrase repeated again and again in an effort to empty the mind of all external thoughts and aid oneness with the God within the universe. The mantra is often given to an initiate by a guru who matches the mantra to the person for supposed maximum effect.

Mass incarnation

New Agers say that at this point in time the Christ is coming alive in all humanity (see **Christ Consciousness**).

Maya

The physical world is seen as only an illusion, a projection of consciousness known as Maya.

Medium

A person who is sensitive or open to be used by occult powers to the extent that they convey information from these powers to others. In spiritism, the communication is supposed to be from dead people, via the medium, to living people. A mental medium will transmit only messages, while a physical medium will attempt to use meditation and forms of physical manifestation.

Metaphysics

When used as a New Age term, this refers to a philosophy of principles applying to the supernatural.

Monism

Refers to the philosophical theory that everything in the universe is essentially the same and therefore should be seen as 'one'.

Mysticism

Belief that God is so outside the range of human logic and understanding that one must approach him with an empty mind and experience spiritual union through an intuitive sixth sense.

Naturalism

Belief that nothing except nature is real and humans are only a part of nature.

Necromancy

Divination by consulting the dead; often used in spiritism during séances.

Neopagan

Follower of a western religious system that is outside the major world religions and cults. Neopagan groups are often involved in occult practices and often have links with Ancient Greek or Egyptian religions, witchcraft and ceremonial magic.

Networks

New Agers spread their ideas and ideals through networks of like-minded individuals, informally and loosely linked.

New Age movement

A loose confederation of people who believe the world is on the verge of a transformation where people will reject Judeo-Christian values and enter a time of peace and one-world government with the aid of Oriental philosophies and practices.

Nirvana

The final release from the cycle of birth and death into a paradise totally separate from anything physical or material.

Numerology

Divination based on the symbolic interpretation of the numbers one to nine. People's names, birth dates and other significant events are reduced to digits.

Occult

A term used for all practices and beliefs that involve the action or influence of secret supernatural powers or entities.

Om

A word (often chanted as a **mantra**) which refers to Brahma, the Hindu creator god.

Omens

Divination by means of interpreting unusual or uncontrollable events, for example, the flight of birds. It is a form of fortune-telling.

One-worlders

Those who want there to be no division between nations so that power is in the hands of one government (basically the United Nations with more power). They believe this will precipitate the understanding of the oneness of all.

Ouija board

A means of communicating with evil spirits and also demonstrating ESP using a board of alphabet letters and a pointer for the spirit to move. Many people have been plagued with fear, depression, rage, anger, insanity and have even attempted to commit suicide after involvement with ouija. It is to be avoided at all costs.

Out-of-body experiences

Spiritual phenomena where an individual's soul seems to leave the physical body while resting, asleep, near death or in a trance state.

Palmistry

A form of divination. The assessment of personality and foretelling the future by examining hands.

Pantheism

The belief that God and the world are one and the same. 'All is God'—therefore everything that exists is divine. No difference between Creator and creation.

Paradigm shift

A change in world views. The expected new paradigm is a world view based on Pantheism and Monism.

Paranormal

Anything above and beyond normal human powers or senses.

Parapsychology

The scientific study of psychic phenomena.

Past lives therapy

Under hypnosis a person is encouraged to release subconscious knowledge of supposed past lives. Allegedly proving reincarnation, this therapy is said to help the individual understand past mistakes which have led to their present condition and enable them to overcome their Karma.

Pendulum

Heavy object suspended from a string, used for dowsing and for fortune-telling. Sometimes swung over people in supernatural healings.

Percipient

A person who receives telepathic messages.

Perennial philosophy

A view that all religious belief and experience are actually one and the same. The externals may be different, but essentially 'all is one'.

Phrenology

Divination by examining the contours of the skull.

Placebo

In drug experiments, a 'pretend' drug is given to a patient who has no way of knowing if it's the real thing. Subsequent tests have proved that even though it has no ability medically or chemically to alter the physical body, in some cases placebos have had a profound effect because many illnesses are psychosomatic.

Planetary Citizens

A New Age activist group committed to promoting a one-world planetary consciousness worldwide.

Planetisation

A global solution to the many threats to human life is to unify the world into a corporate brotherhood that New Agers term Planetisation.

Possession

Usually used to describe a person who is subject to an extreme form of demonic infiltration, due usually to occult involvement. The Bible doesn't talk of possession as ownership, but as demonisation or having an evil spirit. Both Jesus Christ and the early church on his behalf demonstrated that God has the power to set people free from this kind of oppression (Mt 8:28–34; Acts 8:4–8).

Precognition

Advance knowledge of future events.

Premonitions

Advance warnings about specific events or situations. Sometimes this is clairvoyance or ESP.

Psi

A general New Age term for ESP, psychokinesis, telepathy, clairvoyance, clairaudience, precognition, or things psychic or paraphysical.

Psychic

A medium or channeller. Also refers to unexplained or paranormal events.

Psychic birth

Occult counterpart to the Christian experience of being 'born again'. The individual's consciousness is awakened to acknowledge 'all is one'.

Psychokinesis

Power of the mind to move or influence physical objects. Also known as PK or telekinesis.

Psychometry

Using an object owned by a particular person to read psychic information about them.

Psychotechnologies

Refers to many systems and approaches designed to alter one's consciousness.

Reincarnation

The belief that the soul travels on an endless cycle of life after life in different physical bodies in an attempt to evolve to a state of perfection where further physical existence is not needed.

Retrocognition

Knowledge of past events learned paranormally.

Right brain learning

The right side of the brain is said to be the more intuitive and creative, and therefore right brain learning techniques like meditation, yoga and guided imagery are being introduced by New Agers into schools and colleges.

Samadhi

The ultimate goal of Hindu Yoga, also known as Satori in Zen Buddhism, where the individual enters a state of intuitive enlightenment.

Séance

A group of people gather to contact spirits of the dead through a medium.

Second coming of Christ (according to the New Ager)

Many New Agers relate this to the idea that Christ Consciousness is coming alive in the hearts and minds of people all over the world. Others are waiting for a highly evolved avatar to appear on the planet.

Second Sight

See **clairvoyance**.

Self-realisation

To the New Ager this is all about discovering self-divinity.

Shaman

A medicine man or witch doctor.

Spirit control/Spirit guide

A spirit entity that communicates through a medium or channeller, providing information and guidance while the channeller gives over control of his/her being.

Spiritual hierarchy of masters

A group of highly evolved spiritual masters supposedly now guiding the rest of humanity.

Spiritualist or *Spiritist*

A person who believes in the ability to contact departed souls through a medium.

Syncretism

An attempt to combine all religious beliefs and practices, claiming that they are all really the same and teach one core truth, ie that all people are divine.

Synchronicity

Coincidental happenings given deep meaning as though they are psi phenomena.

Synergy

The New Age belief that in nature all things are designed and work together to create unity and enhance oneness.

Tantra

A series of Hindu and Buddhist scriptures outlining yogic practices and techniques for rapid enlightenment.

Tao (sounds like cow)

The Chinese 'way'. A code of conduct, and the basic principle that supposedly holds the universe together.

Taoism

A Chinese religion and philosophy in which everything in the universe is seen to be constantly in a state of flux held together by the Tao.

Tarot

Divination by card-laying, either with tarot cards or standard playing cards.

T'ai chi chuan

A series of very graceful and precise movements which are supposed to enhance an individual's ability to attune to their vital energy or chi.

Telepathy

Communication between minds using ESP.

Theosophy

A forerunner to much New Age thought, Theosophy is a philosophy founded by Helena Blavatsky. It states that individuals possess latent psychic powers, and encourages the oneness of all people.

Third eye

An imaginary eye on the forehead which is believed to be the centre of psychic vision.

Trance

An altered state of consciousness similar to sleep, usually self-induced, in which the mind rests, leaving the person wide open for the control of a spirit entity.

Trance channeller

New term for a medium who goes into a trance when communicating with a spirit entity.

Transformation

This is central to the New Age. Advocates promote both personal and planetary transformation brought about through gradual realisation of the oneness of all things and individual divinity.

Unidentified flying objects (UFOs)

A phenomenon where flying saucers and spacecraft are allegedly seen and alien beings are contacted. This is sometimes an occult experience and many people who have taken LSD, magic mushrooms, or have had an experience of an altered state of consciousness have had hallucinations of UFOs.

Upanishads

The final section of the oldest Hindu scriptures called the Vedas, it is philosophical literature about truth and reality.

Unity in Diversity Council

A council made up of more than one hundred New Age groups which have joined together to promote global co-operation and interdependence.

Vedas

The oldest Hindu scriptures which include hymns and descriptions of sacrificial rites and ceremonies.

Visualisation

Also called guided imagery, this is based on the idea of 'mind over matter'. People are encouraged to allow their minds to change the material world.

Wicca

Nature religion, like witchcraft. It is not as old as it is claimed, and was founded by Gerald Gardner in this century.

Witchcraft

A vague description of the practice of magic, or divination, by people who may or may not also practise satanism.

Worldview

A common opinion of the nature of reality that provides a conscious or unconscious framework for one's life.

Yin/Yang

These are Chinese names which refer to the two principles which are supposed to govern the universe. Yin is the female, inactive, negative energy force, and Yang is the male active force. Yin and Yang are constantly interacting, and these polar forces control the flow of the universe (the Tao).

Yoga

Popularly this word is applied to a series of physical movements, but it really refers to any system or spiritual discipline where the individual aims to gain control of the physical, the spiritual and the psychic. The goal of Yoga in Indian tradition is to achieve well-being by losing one's individual identity and embracing union with the universal one. It is a religious practice and is not to be seen as an exercise routine.

Yogi

A master of various methods of Yoga who teaches others.

Zen

A form of Buddhism which emphasises the experience of enlightenment that comes from breaking down commitment and attachment to logical, rational and material experiences.

3

Life through a New Age Lens

A woman who had been blind from birth underwent a remarkable breakthrough operation in which she gained her sight. The journalist reporting this amazing story asked the woman if the world she could now see was like that she could only imagine.

'It's totally different,' she explained. 'Before I could see I had to rely on my other senses to build a mental image of things. I could smell, touch, taste and hear but I'd never experienced colour and nobody could describe it to me. I really had no idea how big the world is!'

The Guardian newspaper ran a series of adverts on television to promote the idea that their reporting was well balanced and factual. A skinhead was seen walking along the road next to a city gent holding a briefcase. From one angle the skinhead appeared to deliberately grab the briefcase and push the man over. From another angle it seemed that the skinhead was running from someone or something and pushed the man by accident. Finally another shot showed that above their heads some scaffolding was falling onto the pavement. Seeing this, the skinhead rushed over to the man and pushed him away from the debris, thus saving him from a terrible accident. The caption read, 'It's only when you've got the full picture that you can make up your mind!'

Every single one of us makes decisions and judgements on a daily basis about the things that we come into contact with. Our judgements are based upon our view of the factors involved, and our view is often dependent on who we are as individuals, how and where we were brought up, our past experiences and what we've learned. This is our individual framework of reference, the angle from which we look at life. Without a framework we would be unable to make any decisions for ourselves because we would have nothing 'to go on'. Consciously or unconsciously, we all have a framework which dictates the way we perceive all the things around us and the angle from which we base our thinking. We may deny having thought about this seriously, but nevertheless we all have this 'worldview'.

Society as a whole also functions according to a framework of assumptions and ideas about reality. The corporate worldview shapes the culture and so affects life at every level. In the west, arriving on time for a business meeting is seen as a sign of efficiency, but in other cultures it would be a sign of low rank or servitude. In these cultures the boss who really has authority would be careful never to arrive on time! Before we are able to relate to the customs of different cultures, we have to understand the worldview behind them.

In Chapter 1 we identified that many people are now looking towards a coming age of new spirituality, dubbed the Age of Aquarius. If their marketing is successful, people will be conditioned to see life, the universe and everything in a wholly new way. New Agers are calling for a transformation in the framework of everybody's thinking. They claim that a radical change in consciousness is not only inevitable but essential in maintaining the survival of the planet.

The New Age worldview is a real smörgåsbord. It has many aspects and draws from many sources. Therefore, its influence is extremely diverse and far reaching. Like a chameleon, it adapts to its environment. Because of this diversity, not all New Agers hold to exactly the same ideas, but there are several basic themes and ideals that run throughout the gambit of New Age practices and techniques. In this chapter we will look at the underlying ideas which are common to New Age thinking and compare this New Age worldview to that of the Christian.

All is one

Right at the heart of all New Age thinking is the idea that 'all is one'. This is monism and is found in its purest form in most eastern religions and occultism. Everything that is, is seen as interrelated and interdependent. The cosmos is seen as being pure universal energy or life-force, and everything, be it a rock, a tree, a person or a carrot is seen essentially as part of that same energy. All is one—there are ultimately no divisions, no real differentiations between anything, and any perceived differences are seen as unreal. To the monist, the fact that a person and a Brussels sprout are remarkably different both in appearance and function is immaterial, they would claim that it only appears that way.

Maintaining individual identity is pointless to this

way of thinking. Gone is the more Christian idea that each person is unique, individual and distinctive. All aspects of creation are de-personalised. This detracts from the idea that everything is part of the one. There are no absolutes, no right and wrong. Good and evil are not seen as exclusive opposites of one another but according to the Taoist influence in New Age thinking are said to interact so that there is good in all evil and evil in all good.

This is clearly demonstrated in the popular Tao symbol. The cosmic energy force, or the one, is said to have two polar forces—the Yin and the Yang. The Yin is supposedly the female, inactive, negative energy force, and Yang the male, active, positive energy force. Their interaction is alleged to control the flow of the cosmic energy. The one is also known as the Tao. In further chapters we will explore how this idea has been developed into many New Age health techniques.

The one, within the monist's worldview, has always existed, has always been. Because it is energy, it is constantly able to move and change and flow. The world and everything in it is said to have come about as unmanifested energy (energy without any form) shifted to become manifest. Everything didn't come from nothing, but what was could not be seen because the energy or the one had not yet evolved into any material form. The energy is supposedly indestructible —it has always been and will always be. The form which the energy takes changes over time as it evolves, and so all things are said to happen in cycles. The cosmos itself is predicted by New Age astrologers to be approaching yet another cyclic evolutionary shift, dubbed the Age of Aquarius.

To the monist, a person's life is simply an expression of the cosmic lifeforce. The person is emanated from the one and exists in this human bodily form for a short time until that part of the cosmic energy is ready to shift into another form. Therefore, death occurs to the physical body but the cosmic lifeforce lives on. To the monist there is ultimately no death, and this has led to the belief in reincarnation. It is said that if all physical life comes out of the one energy and returns to it, the energy will then re-manifest itself in some other physical form. The illustration goes as follows: when a single drop of rain falls onto the ocean, it can no longer be seen as an individual drop because the water has merged with the larger mass of water, but soon it will evaporate, it will manifest as a cloud until it condenses to form rain, and a single drop of rain will once again fall onto the ocean. We will look at the implications of the monist's worldview regarding life, death and reincarnation later.

Fundamentally, New Agers believe that all of our problems lie in the fact that our current worldview has excluded the knowledge that all is one. Therefore, they say, we need to be radically transformed in our thinking, taking on a new worldview so that, to quote Led Zeppelin's 'Stairway to Heaven', 'You will know the truth at last when all is one and one is all.'

All is God

All is one. Everything is part of the same oneness. There are no differences, no distinctions between all things, and that includes God. If all is energy and the energy is God, then God is in all things and everything is God. This is the basis of the pantheistic worldview common to many New Agers and found in eastern religions, occultism and paganism. To the pantheist, God is seen as an it, not a he or a she. 'It' is an impersonal energy force beyond personality. Ultimate reality, the sum total of it all, is seen as this 'God' energy force, and the pantheist believes it is in everything. If the sum total of cosmic truth and reality is encapsulated in all things, then everything is seen through the lens of the pantheistic worldview as perfect—perfectly God and perfectly equal. The fact that things do not appear to be perfect does not detract from pantheists' acceptance of this thinking. They would say that appearances are completely deceptive and that the problem lies in the narrow-minded old worldview. To worship anything in the cosmos, be it a tree, a snail, a book, a person or the sun, is to worship God.

We are God

All is one, all is God, all is perfect, we are perfect, we are God. For too long, so New Agers tell us, we have been suppressed, denied the realisation that each of us is God. Inside every person is the divine, just longing to get out. Only ignorance has prevented us from completely embracing our individual divinity, and in our ignorance we have suppressed the inner abilities to know everything, do anything, and to overcome all things. Hindus would express this by saying, 'Atman is Brahman'—the individual self is the universal self—and this, coupled with the classic occult view, 'as above, so below', has led to the New Age teaching that there is nothing the individual cannot achieve. 'Unlock your true potential,' for all truth and reality come from God and you are God. So Shirley MacLaine, actress, writer and New Age evangelist, stands overlooking the Atlantic ocean from her beach house and proudly chants, 'I am God'—perfect love, perfect wisdom, perfect understanding, perfect intelligence. To the New Ager, if we are God then we can do anything, including creating our own reality. We are truth, therefore whatever is true for the individual is true, so there are as many realities as there are people.

David Icke is a classic example of the dangers of this kind of thinking. Tragically, in his search for a cure for the rheumatoid arthritis that had ended his football career, he abandoned the reality of his situation and listened to the voices of channelled spirits who led him to the ultimate deception: 'You are God.' So, dressed in a turquoise tracksuit (to symbolise love), he can be interviewed by Wogan and proudly announce that he is God, Jesus reincarnate.

Paradoxically, although the New Age worldview would seem to elevate the individual from 'ordinary human being' to God, in reality, realising that everyone is God and that God is an impersonal energy force rids the individual of his or her unique identity. Don't feel inadequate. Don't hate yourself. There is no room for poor self-image according to this way of thinking. How can you compare yourself unfavourably to anyone else when essentially you are one? At one level this is a very user friendly philosophy—with no absolutes, no external values to guide behaviour, who can tell you what to think, what to believe, what to do? When you are God, you can make up the rules as you go along!

The drawback is that right or wrong becomes meaningless. Rather like the fisherman who felt that sexual morality was irrelevant. 'After all, human beings are only animals,' he asserted. 'When a dog comes on heat it mates with any other dog that happens to be around. So it should be with humans. Go to bed with anyone you like!' A friend then pointed out to him that if this was true, presumably he wouldn't mind if he came home from work and discovered the milk float parked outside his house while the milkman was inside sleeping with his wife. 'Oh no, that's different!' he replied. The friend then observed, 'Oh, I see. One rule for you and another for everyone else!'

Without absolutes we play God and make up what's right as we go along. Such thinking leads to chaos and confusion. Only Christianity has the liberating moral framework that enables each individual to live with dignity. Created individually, we have the manufacturer's instructions to ensure that we remain in good working order, not scarred emotionally, physically, mentally or spiritually.

If we are all God and can create our own reality, then all of these realities are said to be equally true because they are true for each person who chooses them. Therefore, all beliefs and ideas are true. They are said to emanate from the source of all truth, ie, God, and we are God. Different religions and philosophical beliefs are, according to the New Age worldview, essentially the same, with the same core teachings all dressed up in different practices. The differences only appear different. So the New Age worldview is able to incorporate a plethora of different religious ideas and practices, all mish-mashed together. Syncretism of the highest order!

But are all religious beliefs basically the same? If it is true that at their core there is the same foundational teaching that is championed by all New Agers, then it stands to reason that if we were to look closely and compare the basics of the New Age worldview with that of the Christian, they would conflict only in their outward appearance, in the practical outworking of their ethos. So let's do just that. We will compare the basics of the New Age worldview with the biblical worldview and investigate whether there is a common core.

New Age worldview	Biblical worldview

1. How do you view God?

God is impersonal, with no individual qualities, attributes or separate	God is personal, with a distinct character and personality, separate

distinction from all that is. God is ultimate reality, the one also known as lifeforce or cosmic energy.

and individual, with values, concerns, and the ability to choose and create.

2. What is your view of creation?

There is no distinction between God and all that is. The cosmos emanated from the cosmic energy that is God. The energy manifested into various forms which give the deceptive appearance of being different and separate, but this is short-lived for all is part of the one.

God created all that is, out of nothing. God is separate and distinct from his creation, though creation is sustained by his power. Creation is real and good. It shows the mark of the Creator's personality. Creation is now flawed and fallen, but God will renew it.

3. How do you view humanity?

Human beings, like all things in the cosmos, are in essence God. All is one, all is God. Like ultimate reality, humans are ultimately featureless and impersonal. Individuality is a deception. Humans inherently possess all power, knowledge and wisdom. There is no fixed human nature, since, like the one, it is in a constant state of flux.

Humans are part of the creation, sharing its reality. Human beings have been made in the image of God and are therefore designed to be individuals, distinct from God and from the rest of creation. Humanity is not God.

4. How do you view death?

Since all is part of the one energy manifested in various forms, death is merely the end of that particular illusion of reality. All is divine and is beyond ultimate termination. The deceptive appearance of individuality is ended at death, but ultimately there is no death. The one is immortal and we are the one.

Since existence is finite, there are limits to created existence. One of these limits is death. Death, as with other limits to human existence, came about as a result of mankind's disobedience to God (the Fall, Gen 3:14–19). Death is God's judgement on sin—is real and inescapable. Humans die once and face their maker.

5. Can you know God?

Humanity is God. Everyone is essentially united with the divine. We have been unaware of our innate divinity because of social conditioning. We must stop seeing things as individual and recognise that all is one. To know God is to understand your true self.

God created us to have an ongoing relationship with him based on our unique personality and ability to choose it. Our relationship has been broken because we have disobeyed God and actively turned our backs on him. God was prepared to take the first step in settling the problem through his Son Jesus.

6. What is the problem?

Division, anxiety, hostility and conflict have all come about because we have failed to recognise the interconnectedness of all things with the one. We have made the error of thinking reality is finite, and we have been blind to our own divine potential. All problems and negativities can be put down to this basic error.

The problem is that we have gone against the maker's instructions for our lives. We have chosen to turn our backs on God and actively disobey him. Mankind has fallen, and so has all creation. Sin is the problem—it has caused separation from God who is the source of life, health and wholeness.

7. How do you view salvation?

The simple solution is to recognise that all is one and all is divine. Attainment of this knowledge is called enlightenment or God consciousness, and this is salvation, to become one with the one. Enlightenment is very difficult to achieve and requires the individual to attain an altered state of consciousness in order to escape from the illusion of individuality and separation

Salvation can only come as we repair our broken relationship with God. God has made this possible by demonstrating his love for us as individuals by sending his only Son Jesus to bear the punishment for our disobedience on the cross and break the power of death in his resurrection. Salvation is available to those from all that is. Salvation through enlightenment is available to those who are committed to using techniques which will alter their perception of reality. Salvation is the result of perseverance and dedication which finally rid the individual of individual existence.

who, recognising their sin, make a freewill choice to accept Jesus and ask for his forgiveness as the only way. It is the gift of God to be accepted or rejected by each individual.

8. So what's the ultimate goal?

To recognise that everything is interconnected and interdependent because we are all one. We are united with the one and it is our goal to recognise this fully and embrace our union with the one, understanding the implications of our divinity and releasing it.

To restore our relationship with God and live in the good of all that that means: free from guilt; accepted; healed; fulfilled; with purpose and value as a unique and loved individual.

It would appear from this basic comparison of the New Age worldview with the biblical worldview that there is no common ground. New Agers may claim that at the core of all beliefs is the same basic teaching, but this is clearly not the case. We can see that there is more than just a difference in practices and techniques. We have uncovered a clash of worldviews.

Life through a New Age lens is utterly and completely different to life as it appears to the Christian.

Most New Agers claim that 'all roads lead to God'. In real terms that means all roads that follow the path of 'all is one' (monism) and that there are 'absolutely no absolutes'. Tolerance, they say, is the name of the game. Actually, it can be a kind of tolerantly intolerant approach. You're okay if you subscribe to monism: you can believe anything. However if you believe in absolutes, particularly of the Christian variety, you are likely to be ejected from the equation.

New Agers would say that the Christian, biblical worldview is part of the old age, the result of the age of Pisces. Jesus to the New Ager was just one in a long line of spiritual teachers, or avatars, that have come to this planet to teach people how to become aware of spiritual things. 'In the past people needed to be told which way to go, they needed to be led like sheep, but now the time has come for us to make our own way, we can do it, we are God,' explained a self-proclaimed New Age goddess from her home in Glastonbury, where she was filmed for the Channel 4 programme, *The New Age*.

So what is the truth? New Agers would have us think that there is no absolute truth—whatever you want to believe is true, is true for you. But the Bible is quite clear that there *is* absolute truth, and the truth is found in the person of Jesus Christ.

If a friend were to come to you with a tin can in his hand and were to ask you what was inside the can, what would your reaction be? First you would examine the label. For argument's sake, the label states very clearly that this is a can of Heinz baked beans in tomato sauce. But you can't believe everything you read. You examine the label carefully—after all, it might have been stuck onto the can at a later date and the real label torn off. Satisfied that this is indeed the authentic label, you confidently assert that this is a can of baked beans.

Your friend politely thanks you for your opinion but informs you that he believes that it is a tin of peaches. He really believes it and so therefore it is true for him. He is confident that both opinions are equally true because you are both sincerely convinced of it. What do you do? Next step, open the can. It looks like baked beans, but appearances are deceptive, seeing is not necessarily believing. So you smell the contents. It certainly smells like baked beans in tomato sauce but it's still not conclusive. You both taste the evidence. It really is a can of baked beans. Just because he sincerely believed it was a tin of peaches did not alter the absolute truth.

But that's too obvious. How does someone even begin to think about reality in a different way?

A real life example

We have looked at the basic New Age worldview and have seen that it is very different to the worldview common to many westerners. Research has shown that during the teenage years people are more likely to start thinking seriously about the bigger questions of life: 'Who am I?'; 'Where do I come from?'; 'What's it all about?' A friend of ours has allowed us to tell her story and publish some of her diary. It shows clearly how a very ordinary girl began to see life from a New Age perspective while she was still at school.

It was an ordinary November day. Everything was the same as normal. She sat at the very back of the classroom, cross-legged, with a pensive look on her face. With a pencil in her hand, she began to muse about what was to be today's entry in the diary that she had kept so faithfully for the last three years. From her vantage point she could see some of her fellow class mates poring over a teenage magazine. They were talking about what they would wear to the disco on Friday night and giggling over their latest attempts to attract the attention of the fifth year boys from the local grammar school.

How could they be so immature? A rising feeling of resentment began to well up inside her. For almost a year she had been gradually withdrawing from the company of these adolescents, spending every available moment in research. She couldn't remember a time when she had not been interested in the supernatural. Questions about her very existence plagued her mind. There must be more to life than this. So far her research had been restricted to reading books and magazines about the supernatural, but she longed for experience, longed to know the answers to the questions that she was asking. But there was no one she knew who shared these thoughts, no one who would help her to tap into that unknown world, the unknown power source which to many would have been taboo. Everyone seemed so preoccupied with the material world, preoccupied with the surface, the things that they could see.

Suddenly an overwhelming feeling of growing realisation began to fill her. Memories of the last physics lesson that she had sat through flooded back into her mind. Usually she spent such lessons staring out of the window, longing for the bell to ring that would release her from the agonies of all that she found impossible to understand. But this occasion the teacher had been discussing perception and reality. He had explained how the refraction of light alters our ability to see things as they really are. How in various situations we see things and make a value judgement on what it is, its shape and content, and so on, but in reality what we have been looking at could well be just an illusion. She picked up her pencil and began to write in her diary as this growing awareness continued to burden her with the excitement associated with enlightenment.

13th November 1982

Today I have begun to understand something of this incomprehensible thing called life. Now I know why it is that I have been so disillusioned with life as it seems to me, because I really have been disillusioned. What I have seen is not reality, only the surface, only an outward illusion of the truth that is hidden. Finally I am beginning to tap into the truth that is held within us all. The illusion has blinded us all to the truth that only a few are perceptive enough to realise. It is sad that the majority are trapped within the lies that have been fed to them through the centuries. Now it's all coming clear. The people were unable to grasp this reality because their minds had not been enlightened. They had been conditioned to call a spade a spade, and so in order to keep them in line the scholars tried to make it easy for them to understand. They created characters in order to make the concept of good and evil accessible to their shallow minds, so they took one letter out of good and made god and added a 'd' to evil, and so the people were happy in their deception. Now some are able to understand that this is only an illusion, and I am one. I feel so privileged to understand even this little and I long to know more.

She closed the diary, satisfied that at last she was making some progress in her quest for the truth. The feeling of realisation was still surging through her body and she felt strong. She made a resolution. How could she leave these people in their blinded position now that she had begun to understand? Perhaps this was the culmination of the feeling of destiny she had had since childhood. Perhaps it was her mission to bring others to understand the mysteries of reality. One thing was certain, she would never be the same again.

The New Age worldview is available to all who are willing to look at life in such a way that all absolutes are thrown out of the window. It seductively says, 'Anything goes,' wooing the mind with its promise that there can be no one to point the finger of blame. For if there is no right and no wrong, you can make it up as you go along. All is one: all is God, we are God.

It is a worldview that, while bolstering individuals with the belief that they are God, strips them of the dignity of their unique individuality. New Agers are sincere people who sincerely believe that they have found the meaning of existence. Sadly, however, in embracing interconnectedness with the one, they have denied the reality and the value of existence itself.

Despite some positive aspects within the New Age movement, a worldview that has faulty assumptions about existence, reality, God, personality and morality, is an extremely unstable base to build one's life on.

4

P-pick up a Pagan

Andrea and a friend met up with Anna as she walked along the busy high street with her little boy sitting on her shoulders. She'd just come back from spending the winter months in a teepee in South Wales with a group of like-minded neopagans getting back to nature. Carrying a large bag of nuts and vegetables, the staple foods of her vegan diet, she stopped to talk to them.

'Of course it's hard,' she said. 'It's almost impossible to keep clean, and I do worry sometimes that my little boy is healthy out in the elements all the time.'

Disillusioned and hurt by several difficult and broken relationships, she decided to reject her middle-class suburban upbringing. After meeting a man who introduced her to his alternative pagan lifestyle, she and her baby set up home under canvas to face a life of great hardship which she now sees as a small price to pay for becoming one with the environment.

Her arms and legs were covered in huge, pus-filled open sores, and scars of old sores and infected cuts and bites were easily seen. They asked her why her skin was in such bad condition, and she replied, 'It's not surprising, really. We've treated Mother Earth so badly, with pollution and exploitation, and now that we are trying to get back to her, like we did centuries ago, she's reacting out of anger. I've not been living off the land for long enough yet to be used to it. My body will toughen up soon, though, and the earth and I will be more used to one another.'

The evening news was only a low mumble in the background as Andrea and her husband busily tucked into a plate of spaghetti bolognaise. Suddenly they were attracted to a story about hordes of travellers making their annual pilgrimage to Stonehenge for the summer solstice. The police were worried that they would not be able to maintain control, and conservationists were insisting that there should be a four mile exclusion zone around Salisbury Plain to ensure that the area remained intact since some of the stones had been damaged in past celebrations. The scene shifted to London where a representative of the druids and travellers, who referred to himself as a pagan, was lobbying Parliament for the right to carry out the summer solstice ritual practices on the ancient sites.

'It's an infringement of our human rights,' he and many of these pagans or neopagans proclaimed adamantly. 'We want to celebrate this special day and observe the ancient rites. We are pagans. This is our religion, our belief, our right.' The cost of maintaining the exclusion zone and keeping the travellers in order cost the Wiltshire and Hampshire police almost half a million pounds of public money.

A friend of ours came back from a shopping trip in Brighton, unable to believe what he had seen as he had been wandering round the lanes. An authentic Red Indian shaman had been offering his magic art, for a fee, to anyone in need of spiritual enlightenment and counsel for their future life. Gypsy Rose Lee and her crystal ball, a regular attraction of many seaside towns, appears to have been usurped by the increasing New Age trend of looking to the once taboo magic men of ancient cultures for insight.

We have identified that the New Age worldview is being presented as a popular alternative, especially to those disillusioned by what they see as the failure of the material western world to satisfy man's need for spiritual fulfilment. But what is it that could persuade someone like Anna to embrace the kind of lifestyle that our ancestors, no doubt, strived to be free of? Or indeed, what could persuade her that her hideous skin complaint and consequent ill health was only to be expected? The pagan elements of the New Age certainly need to be investigated further.

In search of the great goddess

Not to be confused with Diana Moran (the BBC breakfast programme's ex-aerobic exercise guru), the green goddess, or the army's hospital wagons that come out in the event of an ambulance strike, the 'great goddess' found in pre-Christian nature religion is the focus of many neopagans today.

Once it was thought inferior and uncivilised to be known as a pagan, and even worse to be accused of being a witch. To be a witch has been traditionally associated with wearing a black pointed hat, and anyone with a crooked nose, a black cat and warts has been fair game as the butt of many a broomstick joke. Many have been lulled into believing that witches are mythical creatures that marketeers have kept alive, annually encouraging people to spend their money dressing up like them in order that huge profits can be raked in around Hallowe'en. Yet today you can turn on to one of the many morning TV discussion programmes and very often there will be a self-professed witch being interviewed about the 'ancient art of Wicca', or her views on various subjects from saving the planet through magic to educating children to release their potential energies. And, though their appearance is often mystical and outlandish, they are very keen to steer away from the stereotype of the average child's nightmares.

Thousands of people, both in the USA and Europe, are now proudly calling themselves pagans or neo-pagans. This may be partly due to the studies of anthropologists into the traditional religions and folklore of many native peoples. In a desperate attempt to get away from the modern, material, western world, these new pagans are eagerly accepting a New Age worldview laced with inspiration from Norse, Greek, Roman, Celtic and Egyptian religious practices, plus many rituals and ideas from surviving primal religions.

Interestingly enough, many of the anthropologists responsible for convincing the general public that there were practising covens worshipping the goddess or 'earth mother' as part of a once widely accepted pagan religion, displaced by the onset of Christianity, have since come out of the closet as witches themselves.

Neopagans are keen to give the impression that they are genuinely interested in going back to the beginning, to our spiritual roots, if you like. Yet critics have pointed out that there is no record of such coven activity prior to the fifteenth century. Historical accuracy does not seem to be of paramount impor-tance to the average neopagan. In the words of

Z. Budapest, a practising witch, 'If goddess worship is 60,000 or 7,000 years old, it doesn't matter, certainly not for the future. Recognising the divine goddess within is where real religion is at.'[6]

In trying to get to grips with what New Agers believe, it is important to remember that since their underlying worldview tends to be that there is no absolute truth, not all of them believe exactly the same thing. There are very few 'classic' New Agers. Some have embraced more ideas than others, and there are those who have decided to take one particular route to reach their ultimate goal of spiritual enlightenment. Nicola Beechs-Squirrel, a practising pagan campaigning for nuclear disarmament, gave this statement about pagan belief: 'Paganism is not a dogmatic faith. We have no holy books, prophets or saviours. There is no one true way with paganism, rather a diversity of approach to the faith and a great variety of creative ways in which it finds expression, naturally arising from the infinite diversity of life.'[7] Paganism also has a very interesting perspective on wholeness and morality. As a pagan on the programme *A–Z of Belief* commented, 'Wholeness is to fully express both the evil and the good in us.' A dangerous thing to say! How convenient for those who don't want to say sorry, serve others and deal with their own selfishness.

New Age pagans usually fall within one of the following categories, which we will attempt to outline (some more fully than others): Wicca, Celtic, northern tradition, American shamanism and the Mediterranean tradition.

Wicca

Neopagans are keen for people to accept them as nice, life-loving people who practise legitimate religious rites. They fall over backwards to convince the general public that there is a well-defined line between their activities and those of satanists. Neopagans are interested in utilising religious inspiration from pre-Christian primal beliefs, whereas the interest of satanic covens lies in twisting Christian rituals and belief and turning them upside down. Many modern witches, whose craft is very much a nature-based religion, actually claim not to believe in Satan at all.

It is a sad fact that people are more likely to have read the tabloid press' view of witchcraft than that of the Bible. Few know that the Bible has anything relevant to say at all, let alone about witchcraft, but it really couldn't be clearer in its warning against involvement in the practice of the craft. In both the Old and New Testament, witchcraft is said to be detestable to God (Deut 18:10–12) and is listed among actions of those people who will not inherit the kingdom of God (Gal 5:19–21).

So effective has the witches' publicity campaign been that with little knowledge of their activities, the average person on the street is quick to accept 'white witches' as inherently good.

In the past, according to Wiccans, witches were hunted and burned at the stake because the existing male-dominated society, with their patriarchal religions, refused to accept the goddess. Certainly, there was much mindless persecution in past ages. It could be said that this was more to do with fear, ignorance and prejudice that dominated the society in general, rather than the 'patriarchal religions'.

According to Starhawk, herself a witch,

> The goddess is the world. Manifest in each of us, she can
> be known by every individual, in all her magnificent

diversity. Religion is a matter of relinking with the divine within and with her outer manifestations in all of the human and natural world.[8]

The revival of Wicca, an old English term describing religion and magic, represents the return to the goddess. Pagans hope to be able to create a more positive image of Wicca as a natural spirituality in which the old ways of earth and body combine with ritual and mythology to reharmonise all with the whole, or the one.

The goddess is just another name for the one, who is given a female personality by these pagans. The ancients gave the goddess many names and forms to symbolise their idea that she encompassed fertility, sensuality, imagination and creativity. Whether known as Isis, Diana, Cubele or Hecate, the goddess is being worshipped by increasing numbers of people, particularly women attracted to the mysticism and power offered by those who practise 'the craft'. Witches believe that by attuning to the one, also known as 'kindling the goddess within', they can use magic for their own ends.

Wiccans aim to manipulate the world through their rituals, chanting and meditating to raise psychic energy and release the goddess. Most of these rituals are performed as a group or a coven of about twelve people. The differences between the covens depend on which tradition of witchcraft they follow.

There are the Gardnerians, who follow rituals made popular by Gerald B. Gardner (1884–1964), the 'grand old man of witchcraft'. He saw the craft as a nature religion and encouraged witches, in covens led by a priestess, to worship two main gods: one, the god of the forests and 'the beyond', and the other, the great triple goddess of fertility and rebirth. Gardnerians are known to practise raising occult power in rituals of dancing and meditation inside a circle. In 1955, Gardner claimed to have discovered covens in Britain which had been practising for centuries. This led to massive interest in witchcraft and many new initiates into covens. Yet it is more likely that he did not in fact find these ancient covens, but made the whole thing up!

Then there are the Alexandrians, who came out of a coven started by an Englishman called Alex Sanders. Alex claimed that his grandmother initiated him as a witch in 1933.

And there are those in the Dianic covens who claim to adhere to the rituals of the ancient Dianic cult, much of which was uncovered, so they claim, by anthropologist Margaret Murray, herself a witch.

So-called patriarchal religions, particularly Christianity, are blamed for pushing God from the earth and from the heart of man up into the clouds, where neopagans claim that as a masculine domineering and distant deity he crushed femininity through the exploitation of women and the land. Wiccans claim that Father God has stolen the throne of Mother Earth, the goddess, and in doing so these Wiccan New Agers tend to advocate the superiority of women. Goddess religion is gaining credence among many active feminists. After all, what better symbol of the struggle to overcome male oppression than the goddess of ancient cultures who in all her many guises champions the liberation of each individual from powerlessness? Witches are seen as the ultimate expression of female power and the most positive image of women.

Yet how positive can it be for women, or indeed men, to be associated with something so blatantly dependent upon the manipulation of one sex by another? Insisting that the balance of power be shifted, those worshipping the goddess do nothing for equality, and although some branches of neopaganism do recognise a 'horned male god', it is very clear that their emphasis, and particularly that of Wiccans, lies in the recognition of and reverence to the mythical earth mother goddess.

It needs to be pointed out, especially for the historians among us, that there have been female gods worshipped in past religions. However, they were not necessarily dominant, but by their own admission solid facts are not that important to neopagans. Though their rituals are not the same as those of the ancients, they claim that by creating new rituals they are more easily able to come to a deeper experience of power as they attune themselves to the earth.

It seems strange that these neopagans have rejected the Bible's heavenly Father, totally misunderstanding that he created men and women in his image as equals. In accepting a mythological goddess, who in essence is an ethereal energy mass to be manipulated through strange and secret rituals, these neopagans miss out on the opportunity of a relationship with a God who cares so deeply for those he created that he didn't just sit on a cloud twiddling his thumbs when he saw his children in trouble; he became a human being himself in order that he could provide the way for all who choose it to be brought back to complete fulfilment, knowing God, free from the past and whole in body, mind and spirit.

For God loved the world so much that he gave his only Son so that everyone who believes in him shall not perish but have eternal life. For God did not send his Son into the world to condemn it, but to save it' (Jn 3:16–17, TLB).

The Celts

There is a shop in Chichester devoted to trinkets from the past. It is not a junk shop, nor is it one of the many small and exclusive antique shops. Instead, it sells modern replicas of jewellery and art from centuries gone by as 'the perfect gifts for any occasion'. There is a particular emphasis on traditional Celtic designs spurred by the interest of neopagans attracted to the creativity, mysticism and intricacy associated with that period in history.

In getting back to nature, many have sought to get back to their own historical roots, labelling themselves Irish, Scots or Welsh pagans, and this has no doubt been the motivation which has led to the retreat of many to the hillsides of their ancestors to live out the Celtic life to the full.

With annual pilgrimages to ancient Celtic sites such as Glastonbury, Stonehenge and Lindisfarne, which it is claimed are joined by ley lines of intense psychic energy and spiritual power, neopagans embracing the Celtic tradition believe that all of nature is to be worshipped as divine. They may talk of the goddess as would Wiccans, or refer to the earth by another name, whether it is Gaia, Freyja or Terra, but in its simplest form Celtic paganism has a pantheistic worldview—all is God—and it manifests itself in a variety of forms, or in particular sacred sites. Therefore, it is okay to worship the sun, the moon or any other aspect of nature as it is all ultimately connected to the one.

The fictitious Celtic life of cartoon characters Asterix and Obelix seems to have more to do with hunting enormous wild boar and fighting off the advances of the Roman army than eating lentils and sitting in teepees worshipping trees. However, the druid Getafix, in his obsessive occupation of collecting mistletoe to make the unstoppable magic potion, perhaps gives some insight into what druids do when they are not queuing up to get past the exclusion zone around Stonehenge. Incidentally, getting-a-fix is very much part of the neopagan lifestyle, and the use of drugs is not just common but an essential part of filling the spiritual void and altering the conscious mind to accept and experience mystical occult phenomena.

Neopagan travellers move from sacred site to sacred site to appreciate and attune with these places of spiritual power because they believe man has a great affinity with the earth. The Celtic travellers claim that much of modern man's frustration and stress is caused because we have failed to recognise our inbuilt wander-lust. They maintain that pagan man is designed for the nomadic lifestyle, wandering across the land and living in close harmony with it. A two-week package holiday to Torremolinos is unlikely to scratch the true neopagan's itchy feet.

Northern tradition

Pagans who follow the northern tradition have looked to the Norse lands for their inspiration. Apart from the famous Kirk Douglas/Tony Curtis movie, *The Viking*, in which Douglas' eye is pecked out by a falcon and where Tony Curtis narrowly escapes being eaten alive by enormous crabs, the most well-known Viking is Noggin the Nog. However, many are fascinated by the notorious Scandinavian wild men and by the religious rites and beliefs behind the tribes that built elaborate long boats, filled them with provisions, sent them out into the deep fjords, and burned them, along with the already dead body on board, in order that he or she would be equipped for the 'next life'.

Rune stones, once used by Norse men as a tool to divine the future, are now easily available, and the 'wonder of Rune Lore' is offered to all who are willing to fill in the coupon found in a reputable Sunday supplement magazine. Neopagans are interested in rediscovering Norse mythology and legend, combining this with rituals old and new to create a new blend of paganism.

The American connection

Only a few hundred years ago, white Americans were so afraid of Red Indians and the threat of being scalped that they would drive their wagons into a circle to try to protect themselves, shooting wildly at their brightly painted and feathered enemy as they tried to duck their arrows. Today the great great grandchildren of these early pioneers are back in circles, the difference being that these are medicine wheels, and they are sitting with their old enemies in order to learn from their culture and particularly their native healing methods. Medicine wheels are circles ritually marked out on the ground, sometimes with stones. They are positioned in areas thought to be of particular psychic significance. People are invited to sit inside these wheels that are thought to promote specific healing for individual ailments, as well as having supposed benefits for the earth as a whole.

Since the mid-1980s, the shamanic practices of the north American Indian healers have received much public interest, and a popular pilgrimage for today's neopagans is to the wilderness, fasting and meditating under the instruction of a shaman in an attempt to receive power in visionary experiences. Once, shamans were the taboo magic men whose occult activities were feared and rejected, but in an effort to get back to the old ways of the earth and man's spiritual link with it and the cosmos, these shamanic 'witch doctors' are being drawn out of the woodwork and are travelling from their native homelands to teach prospective shamans and interested New Agers their art, sometimes as far from the prairie lands as the Brighton lanes.

In researching reasons why this branch of the neopagan movement is so popular in the United States, some have speculated that because the population is made up of displaced and often refugee peoples from around the world, there is now a need for them to look for their roots in ancient civilisations.

Shamans and shamanism have been made popular by the writings of people such as Carlos Casteneda and Professor Michael Harner, an anthropologist who himself claims to have been initiated as a shaman through visionary experiences he had while studying the Sioux and Jivaro Indians. Michael Harner now gives lectures and shamanistic workshops, and, along with his tapes of Indian drumming, which supposedly help to send a prospective initiate into 'easier and more sustained' trance states, he is helping to promote the interest of neopagans with commercial success.

Shamans are often people who, having had a near death experience, recover to find that they have the powers to travel into the spirit world, usually in the form of a bird of some kind (they discover which 'bird' their soul represents during a trance). Shamans are then able to prophesy future events and perform healing rituals in which they 'eat' the spirit causing the sickness.

Back in 1890, the shaman Wovoka prophesied that 'the great spirit' wanted the Pauite, Cheyenne, Pawnee, Witchita and Sioux tribes to perform a 'ghost dance' ritual, promising peace and their healing from the results of epidemics and malnutrition. Unfortunately, the US Army, watching from a distance, mistook this for an uprising and massacred hundreds of Indians, something the great spirit obviously overlooked.

The med

The Mediterranean tradition of neopaganism relies heavily on a creative mix of the influences of Egyptian and Gnostic beliefs and rituals. The Gnostics created a problem for Christians from around the fifth century and twisted the teachings of Jesus Christ. These Gnostic or secret gospels are still inspiring neopagans to believe that before Jesus began public ministry at around thirty years old, he travelled to the east where he studied to be a guru under the strict training of yogis and avatars. There is no evidence for this, and the many cults that have taken this myth and incorporated it into their belief system do so, not because they are sure that it is the truth, but in order that they can incorporate eastern mystical techniques and practices under the respectable banner of 'Christianity'.

Few people have never heard of the curse of the mummy which, it is claimed, struck those who disturbed the tomb of the ancient king Tutankhamen. The ancient Egyptians were full of superstition and relied heavily on occult practices and magic in their worship of a whole host of different gods and goddesses. Their pre-occupation with the after-life and belief in reincarnation led them to build enormous pyramids whose shape was believed to have great spiritual power and promote the release of cosmic energy. They filled these gigantic tombs with all kinds of treasures: gold and gemstones, and even food because they believed the deceased would need it when he or she revived. The body would be painstakingly preserved with special balms and wrapped tightly in bandages to prevent decay.

TV presenter Loyd Grossman went *Through the Keyhole* into the home of football star Oswaldo Ardilles and discovered that in almost all of the rooms there was a pyramid. Today many New Agers have pyramids in their homes, cleverly marketed as 'beautiful ornaments which promote healing and well-being', and some have larger pyramids designed for meditation. New Agers believe that sitting inside a pyramid shape while meditating will increase the individual's awareness of the one and help to release potential psychic energies with the goal of attunement, balance and health. Pyramids may well be aesthetically pleasing to the eye, but as for pyramid power, this clearly relies heavily on a New Age worldview and as such is opposed to the biblical standpoint of the Christian.

Whether the New Age pagan would identify him or herself with one of these categories or not, it is clear that there are many common features of neopaganism.

It is sad, though, that while there is an increasing urgency for people to find spiritual fulfilment and something more meaningful than materialism, people like Anna are being deceived by the lie that the earth is a god and robbed of the meaning and fulfilment that they so desperately need. Anna is a victim as her skin decays, her health disintegrates and her pagan immorality leads her to the insecurity of chaos and confusion. She continues to campaign for peace and freedom with a worldview which ultimately can offer neither, since peace is not just the absence of war and freedom and can never be found through a legalistic system of myth, superstition and ritual.

5

How Many Holes Are in Holism?

Her nose was running. Her throat was so sore it hurt to swallow. A common cold. She felt terrible. The doctor said there was nothing he could do. 'Go home, wrap yourself up and drink plenty of fluids.' What was it they said? 'If you go to the doctor's, a cold will only last fourteen days, but if you leave it and do nothing it'll be gone in two weeks.' Useless. She'd tried every trick in the book, from hot lemon and honey to gargling with TCP. What next?

Along the high street there was a health food shop. It had been open for about six months, and she had been there to pick up a packet of multivitamin tablets a couple of weeks before. There was bound to be something natural that she could take that would help her symptoms. Browsing through the various pots and potions proved to be quite confusing. Many of the products did not say what they should be used for. How could she be sure to get the right one for her? Armed with about six different packets of tablets and three kinds of liquid drops and linctuses, she sought the advice of the assistant.

'Yes it's very confusing, isn't it?' the assistant answered obligingly as she removed the pendant from around her neck. 'It's so important to get the one that's absolutely right for you,' she said, taking the girl's hand and turning it palm upward. Deftly, she swung the pendant over the girl's palm and then turned her attention to the bottles that were lined up on the counter in front of her. Holding the pendant over them systematically, the girl watched as the pendant twitched whenever it was over one particular pot of tablets. 'So many people end up relying on the price tag to guide them as to which one to buy, but it's such a false economy. Dowsing is by far the most reliable method.' The assistant scooped up the chosen pills and popped them into a bag. 'These will do the trick!' she promised, holding them out for her customer to take, but there was no one there. The girl had fled. After all, a common cold will only last two weeks!

A New Age for medicine?

We have found that it is in the area of health that most people are likely to come face to face with New Age thinking. It is necessary, therefore, for us to plot the progress of the New Age in medicine and to see how and why its philosophy and techniques are gaining credence worldwide.

But the whole area of New Age health care and holistic practice is enormous, and it would be impossible for us to include an exhaustive list of the many techniques that are currently available to the general public. For this reason, we have included a recommended reading list on the subject at the end of this chapter.

Later in the chapter we will concentrate on a few

of the more widely used techniques that stand at the forefront of the alternative health menu, and we will be asking questions about the scientific grounds on which these practices work. We will be looking at the most common reasons why people today are seeking alternatives for their health, and asking, 'How whole can holistic techniques leave us?'

But before we can approach this thing called New Age medicine and begin to get to grips with it, we need to look at the environment into which these eastern techniques and philosophies of health have come.

Medicine demystified

Until recently no one would have dreamed of arguing with a doctor. They were given an almost god-like status. Today, things are very different. It is common for people to seek a second opinion. The average person on the street has far greater access to information about his or her body and the diseases that can afflict it. The medical profession has to a large extent been demystified, and now it's up for criticism.

Money's too tight to mention

The news is full of stories of cutbacks to the National Health Service. Measures are always being promised to help relieve the enormous waiting lists of surgeons, and heart-rending stories of desperate people needing treatment but unable to get it fill newspapers and magazines alike.

Back in the 1940s, the British government thought that if it spent a large sum of money providing health care for the nation it would be able to control and irradicate the major killers of the time and the nation would be healthy. Health was seen simply as a matter of being without disease, and it was presumed that the cost of providing health care would decrease dramatically as a result. Fifty years on, antibiotics and vaccinations have prolonged the average life expectancy and scientific research constantly widens the scope of available treatments. We have the technology, but technology costs money and priorities are always determined by how much money is in the kitty.

What is health? How can it possibly be measured? People may look healthy on the outside. They may have no real symptoms. And yet they may drink to excess, smoke heavily, eat predominantly fatty and starchy foods, take no exercise and feel generally lousy. There is no disease present as yet, but is the person healthy?

Man or machine?

Man is a bio-psycho-sociological being. We are body, mind and spirit. The World Health Organisation made this statement in 1947: 'Health is a positive state of physical, mental and social well-being, not merely the absence of disease and infirmity.' As such, in order to assist the individual to a position of health it is necessary to look at all aspects of the person's life and lifestyle. Prevention is always better than cure. In practice, though, the majority of people will only consult a medical practitioner when there is something physically wrong. Your local GP is usually so snowed under with patients that in order to make an appointment with the doctor, a person is subjected to a near grilling from the receptionist as to the nature of the problem. It's difficult to get a doctor to visit you at home any more; they simply haven't got the time or the resources, and in many cases, if your complaint is not deemed as a priority you may have to wait over a week before seeing a doctor at all.

Western medicine is criticised for taking the responsibility for health away from the individual and overriding the body's own mechanisms with artificial medications. Doctors are blamed for seeing the patient as 'an illness', losing the person's individuality and dealing with the specific area of malfunction. Mrs Smith in hospital bed 'A' becomes Mrs kidney stone. She is being treated for one specific reason, and once that problem is combated she will leave and Mrs gall bladder will take up residence. People are no longer satisfied to be treated like pieces of meat. Even the label 'patient' has negative connotations as it implies sickness, so many are preferring to be known as 'clients'. A client receives a professional service and is always in control of the situation, actively participating in a relationship of mutual power.

Under pressure?

There has been an increasing move towards encouraging people to be 'health conscious'. There has been a revolution over the last twenty years in people's attitudes towards diet and fitness. At one point the streets were lined with joggers of all shapes and sizes until the man who popularised the sport collapsed and died of a heart attack in Central Park, New York. Yet magazines are full of regimes for those determined to fight the flab, and countless ex-models and actresses have turned to the lucrative market for exercise videos.

Stress has been identified as one of the leading causes of ill health worldwide. The list of stress-related problems is endless, from asthma and eczema, to stomach ulcers, migraine headaches and constipation. More working hours are lost due to stress-related illnesses than for any other reason. Everyone has stress, but not everyone suffers from it. There are different levels of stress, but it seems that different people have different thresholds of coping with it. We all know at least one person who falls apart when even the slightest thing goes wrong or when faced with any type of challenge. We also know others who seem to thrive on it, leaping from deadline to deadline and going from crisis to crisis with seemingly no ill effect. Learning to cope with stress is obviously very important, and many would say that the coping mechanism is the mind.

Valley of the Dolls

Cinema buffs will remember the 1970s film, *Valley of the Dolls*, in which beautiful models who outwardly appeared to have everything became addicted to drugs they believed would help to keep them going when the going got tough. But this situation is not restricted to the world of fiction, or indeed to the lives of the rich and famous. Scare stories of housewives who have turned to their GPs in an attempt to combat disillusionment and stress in their lives and ended up addicted to anti-depressant drugs, unable to function without them, are all too common. The time has come for a whole new approach to health care. A growing number of people are calling for a radical new approach to the subject. If conventional medicine has lost touch with the whole person, it's time that something was done to redress the balance. People are becoming far more aware that they have a spiritual nature, and why should this be excluded from their health care? The New Age has come to the world of medicine, and its answer is 'holistic health'.

It is into this kind of environment that the holistic health movement has taken root.

On holistic ground

It is almost impossible to estimate the total number of holistic practitioners, even in Britain. Almost every magazine or newspaper holds adverts and endorsements for them. The holistic health movement is certainly moving, and very powerfully so. In recent years there has been a total change in attitude towards what was once known almost disparagingly as alternative medicine. It is now more positively referred to as complementary medicine. So radical has the change in public opinion been that the local GP is happy to refer many of his patients to holistic practitioners of many kinds, and even medical health insurance companies will pay out for their clients to receive treatment from healers with no recognised medical or scientific training.

Pain is an overwhelming and incredibly powerful feeling. It can drive people almost to any length in search of relief. Intense pain robs the individual of his or her life and can bring on an insanity that leaves its victim unable to make rational decisions and judgements. Likewise, when faced with the prospect of an incurable or even terminal illness, an individual in desperation will understandably look for any alternative readily available in the health care market-place. The attitude of the majority of people is very much, 'Try anything as long as it works.' Little surprise that when it is seen that conventional medicine has no known answers, and while the scientists continue to experiment and research, the realm of the paranormal becomes a viable option.

Nature's way?

Many people feel that the problems of life stem from the fact that we have vastly over-complicated things. Yet another negative aspect of the materialistic fast-lane world all around us is that we have lost the ability to look after ourselves naturally. Health care regimes are all about re-educating the body to eat more healthily, and to exercise regularly—re-educating the body to function in the way that it is really designed to. We have fallen into bad habits because of the demands of the western lifestyle. It is logical, there-fore, to assume that there was a time when our bodies functioned normally and naturally without the pollution of chemicals. If we could go back to the basics, retracing our steps, we could start again.

Some would go as far as advocating that everything we eat and medicines that we take for health purposes should be completely natural, raw and unrefined. Unfortunately, in their raw state, many herbs, vegetables and drugs that we would have to take on a regular basis contain poisonous impurities which our bodies cannot deal with.

Age of Aquarius

Getting back to nature can be a risky business. It is for this reason that New Agers are keen that we look at the wisdom of ancient civilisations in order to get back to traditional, 'natural' health care. It is assumed that centuries ago man had knowledge for healthy living through techniques which are in essence a synthesis of various elements of mysticism, occultism, spiritism and animism, combined with concepts which have been discovered by modern paranormal research into altered states of consciousness.

We have already seen how New Agers are promoting the view that we are approaching a cosmic transformation marked by an increasing awareness of spirituality known as the age of Aquarius, This evolutionary idea is central to the New Age endorsement of holistic health. To a New Age health practitioner, the fact that a person has no apparent illness or disease is only the starting point for potential health. A French biologist, Rene Dubos, identifies what he calls 'submerged potential illness' in just such a person. Holistic health practitioners see themselves as promoting good health, not as part of crisis intervention, but in order to prevent the possibility of crisis. No one should be content to live in a neutral disease-free mid-point between vibrant health and terminal illness. We should demand good health as our right. New Agers are quick to point out that this will take the complete participation of the individual. Holistic health is less concerned with changing the way medicine is practised, and more to do with changing the way people think about themselves and their relation to the universe.

Life, health and energy

Energy is the key word of the holistic health movement. There are many different techniques, and their roots lie in the cultures and beliefs of many ancient and modern civilisations, from the ancient Chinese to the Egyptians. Yet they are all linked with the essential worldview behind New Age thinking, and that is that all is energy, all is one. Man is seen as part of the cosmic energy force which, as we have pointed out, has many names and guises. Man is energy evolved in a particular form to represent matter. Life is essentially the movement of the vital energy force, and all illness is seen either as the imbalance of energy that supposedly flows through the body, or is put down as a by-product of the population's unenlightened consciousness. Cure is possible through the manipulation and interaction of the practitioner and the flow of energy.

Similarly, since all is part of the one and is essentially the same as the one, this energy-based thinking leads to the common holistic health idea that the problems of the whole are mirrored and identified in a small part. The micro reflects the macro. In the practice of iridology and reflexology, the practitioner claims that in closely examining one specific part of the body— in this case, the eye and the foot—it is possible to identify the problem areas and potential problem areas throughout the rest of the body.

Disease, as mentioned before, is often seen as a signal from the one or universal intelligence that there is an imbalance in the flow of energy through the body. It is often regarded by New Agers as a test or challenge to one's ability to change both lifestyle and thinking so that they are more harmonious and energy-balanced.

The 'whole' person

Any method of healing can be a holistic one if the practitioner takes into consideration the person's whole life. Conventional or allopathic practitioners have in many cases risen to the challenge of a more rounded approach to diagnosis, and when faced with a person with a bout of stomach flu, they may well be inclined to enquire after the individual's sex life, leaning forward, locking eye contact and asking in a meaningful way, 'What's the *real* problem?' There is an underlying disdain for allopathic medicine, which is seen as the big bad wolf of the health care market, although many holistic practitioners are quick to refer clients back to it, especially in severe cases.

'Try anything. After all, what have you got to lose?' Well, money is the first thing that comes to mind. Holistic health care is not cheap. For some cases it is offered on the NHS, but in order to really benefit from its prevention-rather-than-cure approach it may be necessary to visit the holistic practitioner many times in order to see any tangible return for your money. It needs to be recognised that most holistic therapies are unscientific in nature and as such are potentially dangerous when applied to a serious or life-threatening illness. The Bristol Clinic has recently received much publicity as a result of research done into clients receiving 'natural' treatments and therapies for cancer. A report claimed to show conclusively that there was no noticeable improvement to the condition of the clients, and research indicated that without conventional treatment these terminally ill people actually died more quickly, as well as being several thousands of pounds poorer.

'To die? To sleep? To sleep perchance to dream?'

To the New Ager, though, death is not such a terrible thing, and the holistic health practitioner puts on a very optimistic face when challenged by it. If death is seen merely as the final stage in an individual's evolution, allowing an escape into another life in whatever form, it somewhat loses its hold. If a person is convinced of an after-life, whether that encompasses reincarnation or some kind of amalgamation of the individual with the one, death can be approached as merely a transition.

Dr Elisabeth Kubler-Ross, an expert on the process of dying and bereavement, has added much weight to the holistic bandwagon. She has had experience of psychic phenomena through astral travel and through the teachings of spirit guides to whom she is familiar. She champions the holistic approach to the subject, vehemently advocating that we should change our attitude to death and accept it as a passage to new realms of growth and understanding. However, when approaching something as final and important as death certainly is, we mustn't just think positively with the attitude that if an idea helps one cope with the process it must be okay—we must proceed on the basis of the truth. Let us not be lulled into a false sense of security merely because it serves the purpose at the time.

Prove it!

For many of the holistic practices there is little or no genuine, recognised scientific proof that they work.

Many claim that this is merely because we have not devised sophisticated methods of testing these techniques. They assume that as research into the paranormal continues, we will unlock the secrets behind the wisdom of the supernatural world of ancient cultures, and that these will validate not only energy-based thinking, marrying science with religion, but also will authenticate New Age holistic health techniques which currently rely on the testimony of satisfied customers.

Many scientists who are disillusioned with science have turned to the supernatural realm to find some answers, and as a result of their conversion to New Age thinking they have subsequently stated that they have changed their minds as to the nature of the universe. Sadly, it is to the occult realm that they have searched for answers to the questions they should be asking of the one who made the universe and everything in it.

So why do they work?

Until such a time when it can be proved through medical research that these techniques work because of a recognised physical, biological or chemical change, it must be assumed that they work for one of two reasons.

First, that the problem being treated was in essence a psychological one, so positive counselling and the appearance of a 'drug' or 'practical treatment' meant that the result was attained through the patient's positive belief in the practitioner and their methods rather than the drug or treatment itself. This is known as the placebo effect. Many people seek advice and treatment from holistic practitioners while still receiving treatment from their GP. When they discover that their complaint has lessened or that they have been completely 'healed', they are very often quick to attribute success to the 'alternative' care they received and forget that they were still taking conventional drugs.

Secondly, it is possible that the healing was achieved by very 'natural' means, and that it was the body's own healing qualities, not associated with New Age thoughts of life force or inner energy, that caused the person to recover. Often, the person would be back to health just as quickly even without treatment.

Of course, there is another alternative open to us in considering why many of these unproven non-scientific New Age practices work, and that is through some secret or hidden occult power. It is for this reason that we would be very wary of advising anyone to seek the help of holistic practitioners or therapists who claim to manipulate invisible energy using their hands or needles, electronic equipment or magnets. Equally, beware of those who claim to have or utilise psychic power or extraordinary knowledge or ESP. One should also be wary of any particular remedy that it is claimed will cure anything.

Friends of ours were advised at an ante-natal class that arnica tablets were a wonderful cure-all. How could they ensure that their baby was born on time? arnica tablets. How could they prevent bruising? arnica tablets. How could they make sure that they got enough sleep? arnica tablets. What should they do if they felt really tired and lethargic? You guessed it: arnica tablets, they were told, would do the trick. 'You must make sure not to touch them with your hand, though, or you'll contaminate them and they'll be powerless to work.'

Clearly, in the absence of scientific evidence to support the use of such treatments, one must be aware that because their origin is linked integrally with an eastern or New Age worldview, this must be seen, particularly by the Christian, as diametrically opposed to the biblical worldview.

In this chapter we will look more closely at a few specific holistic treatments whose origins are clearly linked with occult practices. Before we do, however, we need to establish this fact: If these practices cannot be proved by conventional medical and scientific testing, they evidently require the patient to believe that the treatment will work based upon an explanation of the New Age worldview in which they are founded. This now becomes a matter of faith. For the Christian, who has chosen actively to put faith in the person of Jesus Christ as the sure hope of his or her salvation, it is not only dangerous but extremely foolish to apportion 'faith' to something rooted in mysticism outside of God's order presented to us in the Bible. In further chapters we will look more fully at the whole subject of the supernatural realm and the issue of good and evil from a biblical perspective. We hope that we will be able to establish a clear picture for Christian and non-Christian alike so that they are able to make a decision about the origins and spiritual effects of these and other New Age and occult practices.

In summary, holistic practitioners should not diagnose particular complaints unless they have medical training, and many haven't. They should be able to give you a full explanation of why their treatment works, and if this explanation relies heavily on any unproven or mythical area it should be avoided at all costs. Simply because there were peoples who used particular remedies and techniques centuries ago does not mean that they are bona fide. Let us not forget that people died because of the barbaric methods employed by native witch doctors in an effort to cure them. Therapies that rely on altering the individual's state of consciousness are very dangerous and potentially damaging. Plus, we need to remember that just because a practitioner is sincere, this is no guarantee that his remedies are legitimate. Certificates on the wall from bodies other than those of the recognised conventional professions mean little except that they have been trained to think, react and treat according to their New Age worldview.

In an attempt to look without bias at the alternative/ complementary health care market, *The Mail on Sunday* came to this conclusion:

> The most convincing reason for seeing an alternative health practitioner is not that they have a proven record of success, that they are more reliable than the GP or that they give value for money since many are very expensive and require you to visit regularly and often. But they have time and lots of it, and their 'craft' requires that they take long histories of the person's life, their likes and dislikes, their situation and anxieties, etc. There are few people who would not benefit from having time to reflect or talk about themselves with someone who cares (even if they are paid to do so).

The holistic menu

Acupuncture

Thousands of people all over the world are voluntarily allowing themselves to become human pin cushions after being impressed by the incredible claims of the ancient art of acupuncture. Needles are inserted into the skin at points on invisible energy channels, called meridians, which are supposedly linked with internal organs. The needles are claimed to be able to unblock, increase or decrease the flow of this energy, or ch'i, when rotated either by hand or by use of an electric current. These meridian lines were first drawn up 5,000 years ago by Huang Ti, the yellow emperor, who combined his belief in astrology and the Taoist Yin/Yang approach to life with his limited knowledge of the functioning of the human body (dissecting the human body was prohibited). There is no proof that these meridians exist, that there is a tangible energy flowing through the body, or that there is a biological link between these points and the internal organs that it's claimed they control. The only scientific evidence for using needles is in the relief of pain where the nerves are able to be blocked from sending signals to the brain.

Acupressure

Instead of needles, pressure is applied to the same meridian points. This is also known as shiatsu massage. The acupressurist may use hands, elbows, knees, or even feet to apply the pressure, along with an assortment of oils and herbal remedies.

Bracelets and bands, which are claimed place pressure on specific energy points on the body and so ease travel sickness or pain from such things as rheumatism, also come under this heading.

Aromatherapy

There is nothing essentially wrong with something that smells nice. Aromatic fragrances can make you feel relaxed, comfortable and at ease. We know that our sense of smell triggers memories—some good, some bad. For instance, we can start to salivate if we smell particularly good food. Aromatherapy involves massaging, bathing and inhaling with essential oils of various herbs. Nothing wrong with that, except that many of the essential oils on the market claim to be made in such a way as to release the vital energy of the original substance, therefore stimulating and enhancing the body's energy.

Biorythms

Graphs are drawn up, based on a twenty-three day cycle, for physical vitality, strength, endurance, confidence and sex drive, a twenty-eight day cycle of emotional moods and creative ability, and a thirty-three day cycle governing intellectual ability, decision making, memory and learning ability. Based on the individual's date of birth as the start date for these cycles, one is supposed to be able to plot the individual ups and downs of life and therefore make valuable decisions about things such as, 'When is the best time to take a driving test?' or 'How will I be feeling next Tuesday as opposed to last Tuesday?'

Colour therapy

Colour can affect people's moods, perception of temperature and time, and indeed their ability to concentrate. Colour therapists claim that specific ailments can be cured by exposing the body to different coloured lights. Few doctors see evidence to suggest that colour in itself can have such a profound effect on particular disorders.

Cymatics/sound therapy

Comparing the body to a musical instrument that needs to be tuned, these practitioners believe that healing can be enhanced by sound waves. Some would even go as far as playing a didgeridoo over their patient to restore harmony and resonance throughout the body.

Do-in (pronounced dough-in)

A form of ancient Chinese self-massage aimed at preventing disease rather than curing it by strengthening the energy channels or meridians supposedly linked with the heart, lungs, liver, gall bladder and stomach.

Flotation therapy

The patient lies in an enclosed tank of water, twenty-five centimetres deep, in total or semi-darkness and complete silence. The water is kept at skin temperature, and mineral salts are added so that floating is effortless. The theory is that once the brain does not have to cope with outside sensations it will turn inwards, so that the person becomes more aware of inner mental and biological processes. Recently endorsed by Jason Donovan, this technique is dangerous and if undertaken for too long can result in the person losing contact with reality altogether, leading to permanent personality alterations.

Herbalism

For thousands of years, people have recognised that some plants have healing properties which can give relief for a variety of symptoms. It was from this basic study of herbalism that modern pharmacology was born. However, many of the herbs in their raw state are highly poisonous, and only in their refined state are they able to be ingested. There is on the surface very little harm with herbal remedies, unless of course it is claimed that their healing properties are the result of some form of energy, or if the herb has undergone an alteration, change or dilution in some unknown or non-scientific way.

Homeopathy

'Like cures like.' Introduced by Samuel Hahnemann (1755–1843), this is perhaps one of the most controversial of the new medicine techniques, not least because it has been made so respectable due to the patronage of the royal family. Now found readily available on the shelves of most high street chemists and health food shops, homeopathic 'natural' products can be prescribed for a plethora of complaints. But on what basis do they work, and are they really as natural as they claim?

Rebelling against the medical profession, Hahnemann began his own research and discovered that when he took quinine he suffered the symptoms associated with malaria. Although in later experiments this same reaction could not be proved, leading to the conclusion that Hahnemann had in fact suffered an allergic reaction to the quinine. He believed that he was able to treat a variety of illnesses using dilutions of substances which in their full strength would cause the same symptoms in a healthy person. He drew up charts which relied heavily on his understanding of eastern philosophy and his deep interest in the occult and all forms of psychic and paranormal phenomena, and he came to the conclusion that it was in the process of dilution that the power to heal was released from the original substance.

Hahnemann claimed that throughout the stages of dilution as the substance is shaken, a cosmic vital energy force is released, and it is to this 'force' that he attributed the success of his homeopathic remedies. He was particularly keen on a solution so diluted that if tested not even a single molecule of original substance would be found in the bottle of supposed remedy. In short, too little active chemical to do any harm and too little to do any good.

Today, some homeopaths would be reluctant to use quite the same level of dilution that Hahnemann instructed so that their remedies could have some organic effect (although this is very unlikely). And some would openly admit their faith in occult practices, adhering to the idea that there is cosmic vital energy in all things animal, vegetable and mineral and that they are able to release and harness this power for healing.

Homeopathy has been very quickly and easily adopted into the New Age spectrum of treatments, and while it would be comforting to think that it is possible to take natural remedies with little or no physical side effects, until it has been categorically and scientifically proved that cure is rooted in a measurable physical reaction or change within the body, one must assume that the power behind homeopathy is spiritual and has spiritual side effects.

Bach flower remedies are marketed in a very similar way, and you can find small bottles of these remedies in most health food shops. These flower remedies are diluted in solutions of brandy and water and claim to be able to vastly improve, if not cure, conditions such as loneliness, fanatical beliefs, depression and anxiety, as well as a list of physical ailments. How anyone can believe that a few drops of potion will cure the fact that they live alone and have very few friends we are not sure. The potential danger in such cures speaks for itself. 'Cures' which promise miraculous results yet have no real power could prove fatal to those who are desperate.

Hypnotherapy

Used in a variety of treatments from fear of spiders to dentistry, modern hypnotism, pioneered by Franz Mesmer (1734–1814), is still on the increase. Gaining credence with the conventional medical profession as a helpful extra, the patient's conscious mind is put on pause, rather like a video machine, and the subconscious comes 'out to play'. Once in a trance, the patient is able to be manipulated by the hypnotist's suggestions. This only works if the patient is a 'willing victim', completely trusting the hypnotist and allowing him or herself to become like a robot without any control. People have been known to suffer from severe psychological side effects as a result of undergoing hypnosis, and some have been known to experience confusion and personality changes involving uncontrollable laughter, anger and crying.

Mesmer confessed to finding that while he performed his stage act, which involved hypnotising members of the audience, he would find himself overcome by an outside occult power. Hypnotism undoubtedly has many roots in the occult and is an integral part of some witchcraft practices. Many people have claimed to have clairvoyant or psychic experiences as a result of hypnosis, which is similar to a medium's trance.

Hypnotism is an essential part of many New Age practices, including rebirthing in which patients are supposedly able to retrace through their subconscious mind all the stages of their life and before that to past lives, going over supposed events which have moulded and shaped their current personality. Heavily linked with the eastern philosophy of reincarnation, patients are supposed to be able to talk in different voices and take on other characters as though they were someone else in a past time. We are very clear in our view that these are in fact the same phenomena associated with trance channelling or medium spirits which we will be outlining in the next chapter.

Some practitioners claim that hypnotism is purely mental and in no way dangerous. One wonders how they are able to justify this against the evidence to the contrary. Laying aside the dangers of the spiritual dimension involved, it is certainly dangerous to allow oneself to be at the mercy of hypnotists, however bona fide they may seem.

Iridology

Studying the markings on the iris of the eyes and observing changes in them, these New Age practitioners claim to be able to locate and diagnose problems in the body and mind. Conventional doctors do look into the eyes to see indications of specific diseases. However, they would not go as far as iridologists who claim that the iris is like a map of the entire body, and little wonder as this has not been proved to be scientifically correct.

Kinesiology

Kinesiologists claim that each group of muscles is related to specific organs, and that healthy muscles equal a healthy body. They do not diagnose but look for imbalances in energy in the body, testing the reaction of the muscles, their strength and weakness, to pinpoint problems. Kinesiology has not yet been sufficiently researched to give it credence as anything other than an 'alternative' technique.

Reflexology

To the reflexologist, the foot is the mirror of the body. Parts of the sole are said to be connected, via 'energy channels', to other parts of the body. Dividing up specific areas of the feet to represent the different organs, the reflexologists embark on a course of foot massage to stimulate the flow of this supposed energy and move any of the sedimentation they claim has built up and caused blockages for it. No clinical trials have been conducted to prove the claims made by reflexologists, though they continue to market their technique for a variety of ailments, including back problems, migraine, digestive disorders, period pains and stress.

T'ai chi

This ancient Chinese art is based on slow, circular dance-like movements which are best performed in the open air. The basic thinking behind this is that emotional and mental disturbances can cause imbalances in the body's energies so that too much is gathered in one area, such as the head or the chest, and too little in another. These imbalances are supposedly corrected by concerted mental focusing through a series of precise movements. A highly complex therapy involving a lot of patience, perseverance and agility, it has to be learned by a qualified teacher because it is a 'growing' therapy whose benefits gradually unfold as one learns to focus more fully to become one with your chi and subsequently the cosmic chi.

Visualisation therapy

Based on the belief that mind and body affect each other directly so that thought can have physical and mental effects. Patients are asked to create a vivid mental picture, and this is used to combat their problems. Therapists claim that visualisation is suitable for just about every kind of physical or emotional difficulty and that there is nothing that mind over matter is not able to control. Many are encouraged to see themselves as God, creating their own situations, taking control of the situations that are around them and creating their own reality.

There is nothing essentially wrong with imagining that things are better. There is nothing wrong with being positive and focusing on biblical truth. However, we must be aware that much in this New Age technique promotes the philosophy that we are God and are therefore able to overcome, rather than the biblical worldview in which, as created beings in relationship with God through his Son Jesus, 'we are more than conquerors' (Rom 8:37). Using visualisation to change situations in reality means that participants are endeavouring to use and experience psychic power.

Other New Age techniques available in today's market-place include all sorts of magnetic treatments in which a magnet is swung over the body, particularly over points of pain (such as over the back in cases of acute back pain). The magnets are supposedly able to help rebalance a magnetic field around the body.

There are also aura therapies where an experienced psychic identifies the supposed aura or psychic glow around an individual. These psychics supposedly heal any malfunctions or problems within the body or the psyche through the manipulation of this aura, and they use various methods, including colour therapies, light therapies, laying on of hands under the influence of spirit guides, or the use of strange oily aura potions.

It is certainly true that life in the fast lane has taken its toll on our health. We do need to spend time reflecting on our lifestyle to find where our priorities lie. Are we spending enough time relaxing; exercising? Are we eating regularly and really looking after our bodies? After all, this is the only one we've got. If the New Age has taught us anything at all, it is that we need to balance our lives to cater for the fact that we are body, mind and spirit. Sadly, though, in recognising that man is not a machine and that there are some flaws in conventional medicine, New Agers have introduced techniques and alternatives which have undeniable links with occult, mystical practices and eastern philosophies.

There are so many different techniques available that it can be very confusing, but, as we have already outlined, if you are at all in doubt as to the basis on which any health technique is used, ask the practitioner for an explanation of how the method works. If the explanation sounds at all vague, or if the technique relies on ideas of energy or on any non-scientifically proven methodology, we would advise that you steer clear of it. The majority of New Age practitioners are reluctant to perform their techniques on non-believers anyway, as they feel that the patient must be completely involved in the process for the maximum effect.

The time *has* come for us to have a whole approach to our lives. But more than anything we need to be whole people, and this can only be achieved through proven physical techniques and a spiritual life whose foundation is not full of holes!

Recommended reading on the subject of alternative health care:

Samuel Pfeifer MD, *Healing at Any Price?* (Word: Milton Keynes, 1988).

Reisser, Reisser and Weldon, *New Age Medicine* (InterVarsity Press: Illinois, USA, 1987).

6

New Ideas for Old

New Age on the rocks

It was the height of summer, a lovely night for a barbecue, and at the local open-air museum that was exactly what was going on. As Andrea and a couple of friends queued for their beefburgers (glad to be omnivorous since the veggi-burgers had unfortunately become irretrievably mushy) they noticed a table that was laden with a variety of different gemstones. Fascinated, they took a closer look, only to discover that they were encountering 'the New Age on the rocks'. There were stones of all colours, sizes and varieties, and a covering explanatory notice stood at the side of the table:

> Everything is energy—all is one. Over thousands of years these precious gemstones have captured within themselves the vital energy force that is the essence of all that is. We can release this energy and with the help of these stones restore balance and harmony to our lives, our bodies and all around us.

True enough, the stones were quite pleasant to look at. Some had been crafted into very attractive pieces of jewellery. Yet by the side of each variety of gem there was a small slip of paper which revealed the more sinister side to their *raison d'être*. As they scooped up handfuls of free leaflets to read at their leisure, the woman standing behind the table noticed a ring that Andrea was wearing.

'Ah, malachite,' she mused. 'A wonderful gem. You know, it's so intense, it can help us to break free from so many of the things that limit us like fear and guilt. It can even help us to break old habit patterns and increase courage and determination!'

Walking through Sainsbury's wearing a pair of earrings that Andrea had been given as a present, a local 'occultist' approached her to ask, 'Are they lapis lazuli?' Having read the leaflets explaining that New Agers believe that this stone aids psychic development, lifts depression and gives hope and self-confidence, she was uncertain whether to answer in a quiet and grumpy voice, 'Who said that?'

On the face of it, it's quite illogical to think that sound-minded people can actually believe that these pieces of rock, precious or otherwise, can actively affect their lives, yet in New Age shops all over the country these gemstones and crystals are being marketed as the ultimate aids to 'spiritual' well-being.

On a recent visit to Glastonbury, hotbed of New Age thinking and focal point of many New Age pilgrims, it was clear from even a cursory glance in the local shops that gems are big business. From small pebbles to pyramid-shaped crystals. From pendants to large mounted pieces of precious rocks.

It's sad that these very attractive pieces of God's creation are being assigned such 'spiritual' significance in the New Age worldview. Some would even go as far as saying you don't choose your crystal, it chooses you. Subconsciously, they explain, you will be drawn to the crystal that is supposedly resonating at the same energy frequency as your own body force and therefore it will be more effective in aiding your spiritual growth and development! Crystal jewellery is becoming very popular. However, when crystals are worn for anything other than aesthetic reasons one must beware.

Taking the New Age philosophy of universal energy to its ultimate end, there is little reason why anything shouldn't be marketed commercially as an aid to balance, harmony and focus. Greengrocers could become healing centres if carrots 'full of the force' and cabbages 'encapsulating the one in each leaf' were to be hyped at the same pitch. However, it is these gemstones which are the latest New Age hot cakes and large amounts of money change hands every week while people are deceived into thinking that these stones will solve their problems for them.

Forgiveness and friendship are said to be the by-products of rose quartz for those attuned to it. Clear quartz is said to 'help extend your aura, giving extra protection against modern negative energies such as the electromagnetic fields surrounding fluorescent lights, televisions, radios or microwaves'. Some stones are supposed to be particularly effective on certain parts of the physical body, helping specific diseases, although, of course, there is no medically proven evidence that this should be so. There are those stones to be used purely as aids to reaching higher levels of attunement during meditation, and the goal of some New Agers is to project their consciousness inside the crystal itself. Finally, to tiger's-eye is attributed the powerful properties of being able to 'protect from witchcraft and evil, bringing good luck and helping to give insight into the inner self', a dangerous claim!

Unfortunately, New Agers have sold the general public short. No matter how old a piece of rock, no matter what colour it is or how readily light can be refracted through it, according to the biblical worldview, they are just pieces of rock with no spiritual significance other than the fact that they are part of the incredible craftsmanship and imagination of the Creator God.

It is more than dangerous to leave people believing that pieces of stone will help to alleviate their life problems, and tragic that many are duped into thinking that it will cure the pain and guilt of the past and offer forgiveness. Jesus is the only Rock that is able to offer the kind of life and security that these New Agers attribute to these inanimate stones. 'The Lord . . . is the Rock eternal' (Is 26:4); he has become the 'capstone' on which everything else rests and is held together (1 Pet 2:7); and salvation is found in no one else (Acts 4:11–12). You can't get blood out of stones, and no matter how hard you squeeze you won't find forgiveness in them either.

As we look at the New Age with all of its many guises, we are able to see that one thing is clear: people need answers to the questions they are asking of life and there are plenty willing to provide them, at a price—but at what cost?

Old ideas are being dressed up as new ones to meet a world eager for a New Age where the problems of the past are just that. The idea of crystals and gemstones with power is quite literally as old as the hills, and yet it is being pitched as the latest in modern 'New Age' philosophy. As is another New Age craze resurrected from the past, and that is 'channelling'.

Channelling—New Age spiritism

First Tuesday, the documentary programme that covers specific topics of interest on the first Tuesday of every month, was investigating Los Angeles housewife Penny Torres Rubin who was gaining considerable popularity and acclaim for the seminars and workshops that she was holding, not as herself, but as a 'channel' to a disembodied entity named Mafu.

This petite and very feminine blonde voluntarily allowed her whole body to be completely controlled by this spirit who claimed to be a 'member of the brotherhood of light' in the 'seventh dimension', and in doing so she changed completely. So convincing was her performance as Mafu that her voice, personality, movements, gestures and speech patterns were completely different from her own. Mafu, a very masculine, powerful character was now able to conduct seminars, teaching willing students all they might want to know about reality and the world beyond the physical realm. Laying hands on some of those who had paid a considerable sum to be part of this exclusive class, Mafu gave direct words of 'encouragement' and displayed supernatural knowledge of individuals' lives, with a basic message: 'You don't need anyone to tell you what to do—you have everything that it takes. Indeed, you are able to create your own destiny, shape your own reality. You are God!'

Penny Rubin, convinced that the entity that channels through her is bona fide, claims that she is able to leave her body completely while Mafu enters. She explained to the TV presenter, amazed at what he had just witnessed, 'If this is just me and somehow I am able to make this up, if this is just a performance—I want all the credit. I must be incredible!'

'Everyone can channel'

Channelling is spiritism New Age style. Formerly, mediums were those who sat in darkened rooms and received messages from 'beyond the grave', from spirits tormented by the need to communicate with their loved ones. But things have changed, and so has channelling. Once thought to be a gift that only a few were blessed with, the New Age message is that everyone, young or old, related to gypsies or otherwise, has the potential to be a medium or channel and receive revelatory information from a supernatural source. Gone is the stereotypical parlour séance and the quiet personal reading, although they are still very popular. Instead, the 'spirits' are preferring to go public, holding seminars and workshops for large audiences, even appearing on radio and TV talk shows, answering questions and giving advice.

But just what is being channelled? Who or what are these entities? And why is there so much controversy over channelling, its purpose and origin, even among the New Age community?

Knock, knock, who's there?

Historically, it has always been channels or mediums who have gained public recognition for their ability to contact spirit entities. Doris Stokes gained a huge following and made a very good living for herself holding public séances and writing several books about her experiences as a medium. But recently the entities themselves have been reclaiming the ground, and in some cases they have even become more well known than their channels.

In a recent award ceremony in the USA, the actress Sharon Gless, of *Cagney and Lacey* fame, publicly sited Lazaris as the driving force behind her successful career. Thanking him for his support and encouragement, many would have been unaware that Lazaris is in fact a disembodied entity who has been channelled through Jach Pursel since October 1974.

In the 1930s, a group of anonymous writers published the *Urantia Book* which told of 'ascending universes and evolved beings'. Recounting the histories of Urantia (supposedly the earth) and gnostic information about Jesus, this book had been completely channelled by spirit entities through automatic writing. Since then, several spirit entities have gone into print, and channelled literature is gaining increasing popularity.

Some claim that these channelled entities are highly evolved beings, enlightened ones whose aim is to communicate with human beings in order to aid our evolution. Some entities tell elaborate stories of a past physical form, giving 'proofs' of their past existence. Interestingly enough, there are entities claiming to have been everything from Merlin the Magician to lowly servants in Pompeii prior to the volcanic eruption. Kevin Ryerson, famous for being instrumental in Shirley MacLaine's initiation to the New Age, claims to channel disembodied spirits who, in between incarnations, are keen to play their part in making the earth a better place for them to return to. And there are those entities who would claim that they have never been part of this physical realm, but rather have remained as spiritual beings in another dimension, or indeed have inhabited another solar system. Some channels, Uri Geller being one, are actually claiming to be able to communicate with extra-terrestrials from the future!

Spirit communication

There are several different forms or methods of channelling. Clairaudient mediums or channels remain fully conscious as they repeat what the spirit entity communicates to them telepathically. Some would say that their body is controlled by a spirit and that it communicates through automatic writing or through manipulating communication instruments like the ouija board or pendulums. Some channels claim to experience a kind of 'half trance state' in which they remain only partially conscious while the spirit entity manipulates the channel's voice in order to communicate. The channel would then have some memory of what has occurred during this experience. But those like Penny Torres Rubin, who go into a deep trance state while channelling their familiar spirit, have no memory of what occurred while they were unconscious. Jach Pursel, who channels Lazaris as a full-time career, can spend up to forty non-sleeping, unconscious hours per week giving over complete control to the entity as it conducts lectures and seminars. This full body incarnational channelling could to the cynical appear to be just a 'convincing performance' on the part of the channel because there is no inhibition on the part of the spirit: it is able to use the channel's body to its full extent, interacting with its audience, and walking and talking with no problem at all.

Channellers claim that what they are doing cannot technically be called 'possession' since they are more than willing for the spirit to enter their physical body completely. Yet from a biblical viewpoint, this is clearly what is taking place as these entities give extraordinary demonstrations of supernatural power and revelatory knowledge as 'hooks' to an audience willing to comply, unaware of the real implications of their occultic and anti-biblical teaching.

Higher self

Shirley MacLaine is among those New Agers who claim that they are able to channel their higher self— that most spiritual knowing part of oneself, beyond the day-to-day conscious ego, also known as the god or goddess within—and that it is the higher self, given a character by our imagination (in order truly to reflect who we supposedly really are!), that is able to guide us and impart wisdom. Shirley, however, is also very keen to follow the advice and spiritual guidance of other channelled entities, even though they claim not to be the higher self, but if all is one, what does it matter what the entities individually claim to be, or indeed what you might believe they are? This is how New Agers are able to get over the problem of controversy over what these entities really are. It doesn't matter what you believe anyway, so don't let it worry you!

Very fishy!

A current craze among New Agers, particularly in the United States but becoming increasingly popular in Britain, is channelling dolphins. These lovely creatures are believed by some to be more highly intelligent and spiritually evolved than humans, and it is reckoned that by swimming with dolphins and channelling them we can learn from their message of love and world peace. While we would not wish dolphins any harm, and while we think that being able to swim with dolphins would be a valuable human experience (as is contact with any animal or mammal), one must be conscious of going overboard with ideas such as these which are clearly unbiblical and unscientific. Although they are intelligent, exactly how intelligent has not been proved.

Past life?

Some would use the phenomenon of channelling to endorse their belief in reincarnation. Past life recall therapy is used by many New Agers who under hypnosis are encouraged to journey back in time to recall supposed past incarnations as different people in completely different life situations. During these recalls, the 'travellers' can take on completely different personas, voices, mannerisms and genders in their convincing performances of their past lives. Again, giving convincing proofs which cannot be explained (although some have been discovered to have been the result of subconscious memory of history books or stories told during childhood), the New Ager is encouraged to understand that death and life are only parts of the journey to fulfilment, and to take solace in the revelation of who they were and, in some therapies, who they will be.

Ghostly gurus

Interestingly, no matter what they are believed to be, the fundamental message of these entities is in essence the same: all is one, you create your own reality and therefore you don't need to be told anything because the wisdom of all reality is held within. However, these entities are paradoxically still giving out advice and guidance and don't seem prepared to stop while New Agers are more than ready to follow in their wake. Gone may be the era of the human guru, but with the New Age dawns the era of the disembodied guru.

Doorways to danger

But how do people become channels in the first place? Sadly, research has shown that the majority of those who channel spirit entities have either had some form of trauma during early childhood or have taken part in or had some experience of occult practice and phenomena, whether this be yogic meditation or some form of séance. The most common route is through playing with the ouija board, a very dangerous pastime, in which inviting the spirits to communicate can lead to a series of events not bargained for by the player.

A true life story (continued)

Things hadn't been going well. Work was hard and getting harder. Her month's wages had long since run out, and her boyfriend had just given her the elbow. If only she knew for certain that things were going to look up. All she wanted to know was, would she ever be really happy? Would she find someone to love her? Would she ever have enough money to pay the rent?

At first she'd tried reading her horoscope and had progressed to drawing up her own natal chart with the use of a book she'd borrowed from the library. It was mildly encouraging, but it just didn't give her the answers she was after. She'd learned to read tarot cards and had her palm read professionally, yet these were all too impersonal. A friend suggested they contact 'the spirits' with a ouija board, and she was eager to give it a try.

The glass moved, slowly at first, across the coffee table on which they had laid their makeshift ring of letters. Encouraged by her initial success, it wasn't long before she was using the board on a regular basis. Initially, the spirits had communicated by pushing the glass towards the letters to spell their messages, but with each further session the glass had begun to move too quickly for anyone to be able to see what was being said. It was then that she began to hear their voices, pre-empting what they would spell, telepathically knowing what they wanted to say.

'How do I know I'm not just making this up?' she asked herself. 'How do I know they are real?' But the spirits were too quick for her doubts and they soon produced proofs for her, revealing information about people and places that she could not possibly have known, even in her subconscious mind.

One night a spirit who called herself Marjorie introduced herself to her. Congratulating her on her ability to be a channel for communications from the spirit world, Marjorie explained that 'she' needed a physical body to be able to communicate completely with this world. Flattered to have been given this tremendous opportunity, the girl willingly complied, and, lying back, she allowed the spirit to enter her through the diaphragm (solar plexus) which became burning hot to the touch. In a half trance, her breathing completely altered, her voice changed as her limbs became icy cold to the touch, and her eyes, normally grey blue, became a vivid purple colour. Marjorie laughed. She was amiable, telling jokes and amusing the company with her witty anecdotes of the spirit world. She remained there being channelled for about half an hour the first time, and once she had gone the group of people gathered around the girl, wrapping her in a duvet as she shook, elated and sobered by the experience.

In time she learned to channel Marjorie at will, but whose will? If she wore the colour purple Marjorie would 'appear' and talk with her, or through her, or both. At times she worried she may be schizophrenic. If she looked into the mirror, often she would not see her own face but that of Marjorie staring back at her. Sometimes when she picked up a pen to write, Marjorie would guide her hand to write messages and poetry, ruining what she had originally intended to write. Marjorie was not willing to wait to be channelled; she wanted to call the shots, 'You are my channel—it's your duty to be my lips, my hands, my body!'

It was then that another spirit, calling himself Samuel, introduced himself to her. 'I have always been with you,' he told her. 'I have always loved you as I have watched you grow. I am here to protect you and to guide you.' He also gave convincing proofs of who he was, and she wanted to believe him. He was powerful and seductive. She trusted him. Sometimes he would 'appear' to her. Once, he danced with her, swinging her into the air as they danced the polka. Marjorie was too jealous, too possessive. Samuel had warned Marjorie not to spoil things with her negativity. Samuel cared.

She had been told all the things that she had wanted to know, had answers for all her original questions, and now she was being taught more. Sometimes the things that she was told did not come true and she would become confused, but she always went back to Samuel to ask him why. She no longer needed a ouija board, no longer needed the 'props' that she'd thought were necessary in the beginning, although Samuel liked her to cover herself in the colour turquoise. With a mixture of truth and falsehoods, he hooked her. She would consult him before she made any decisions. She trusted him—with her life.

Becoming a channel had been easy. She had been open to the supernatural realm. She had willingly invited these spirit entities to become part of her, to use her as their instrument, their tool, but who was in control now? Gradually, she had abdicated the responsibility for her life to Samuel, allowing him to make the decisions for her, listening to the things he taught her, heeding all of his advice. 'You can do anything! You are special! You can make anything happen! Death is nothing! Death is not real! Death is life! Choose life, choose death! Be with me, we can be one!'

He had told her that he wanted the very best for her, that he would protect her, and now he was advising her to end it all. She woke from a trance with a knife in her hand pointed towards her. Was Samuel so in control of her destiny that he would bypass her will?

Finally, things came to a head. Battling with Samuel about what was best for her life, she was unaware that fifty miles away her cousin and a couple of other Christians were praying for her, praying for God to break into her life and reveal the truth to her, reveal himself to her as the one true God. One night in March 1986, Samuel came to her. The room was full of people; the atmosphere electric. 'Now,' he said, 'now I have you. You are completely in my power; completely mine. You are trapped; nothing without me. You are mine!'

She stood to her feet, frightened, confused and angry that this spirit she had trusted could have completely deceived her with his subtle lies and seductive charm, and, with a voice that seemed to come from deep within, she screamed, 'You will never have me—because I've got Jesus!'

God's communication channel

Channelling is not God's intended means of communicating with his people, and these channelled spirits are not to be confused with the Holy Spirit. The Bible is very clear that communicating with these malevolent spirits, however they choose to disguise themselves, is detestable to God (Deut 18:10), no matter how convincing their 'proofs' may be (Acts 16:16–18). Saul lost his kingdom because he chose to consult a medium for the answers that he wanted, instead of trusting God (1 Chron 10:13–14).

God speaks to his people through the Bible, which is the inspired written word of God—not a channelled work of automatic writing, but compiled by a number of writers who from their individual perspectives and situations and in their conscious mind were inspired by God to write about events and explain the outworking of God's plan for his creation.

When God speaks his prophetic word through his people (1 Cor 12:4–11), it is God speaking by his Holy Spirit and not another 'spirit'. God speaks in order to edify, encourage and exhort his people with the purpose of bringing them into closer relationship with him through his Son Jesus. His prophetic word never contradicts what he has already revealed as his will and purpose in the Bible.

From a biblical viewpoint, these channelled entities are deceiving spirits or demons, fallen angels who were banished from the realm of God's kingdom when they disobeyed God's authority along with Lucifer/Satan, their commander-in-chief. Their purpose is to deceive and manipulate those who will give them ground, in order to beguile with their heretical philosophies and keep people from having a relationship with the only true living God.

It is a strange paradox that while New Agers claim not to need any outside authority, and while they insist that there is no need for them to follow any particular guidance, they willingly accept the messages of channelled entities as though they were scripture. They will read anything that has been written about the spiritual realm by occultist channels and mediums, whether it has been directly channelled or not, yet they will not accept the authority of the Bible and its guidance or advice. Insisting that the Bible cannot be relied on to give a true picture of spiritual reality, the paradox is that the New Age message proclaims that there is no truth. Basically, anything is okay so long as it's not the Bible in its literal translation. Anything, so long as it doesn't place any moral demands on its followers.

So popular has the idea become of being able to have spiritual advice without moral demands that every day, all over the western world, people are turning to horoscope pages in the newspapers and seeking the guidance of the zodiac. Another ancient art has been marketed commercially for the New Age, and that is astrology.

Reach for the stars/New Age astrology

The Brighton Festival radio station was doing a show about astrology, and those who worked there invited Andrea to take part in a panel discussing the pros and cons of this popular phenomenon. Professional astrologer, Errol Masters, and a woman who regularly uses astrology were to put forward their case by claiming that astrology is a harmless and beneficial tool that can help people to understand themselves more fully and allow the individual to be able to make life decisions freely. They were clearly not prepared for the response they were to be faced with.

Astrology has gained a respectable face. Asking people what star sign they are is acceptable small talk. Gift shops are full of personalised zodiac mugs, key-rings and jewellery, and very few newspapers and magazines will not carry a horoscope column. 'Your week ahead!' 'Your stars!' But few realise that what they are reading is mythology.

Many are quick to point out that some of the tabloid horoscopes are just made up, a bit of a joke by the journalists who throw them together to make last minute copy. But there are those who are very sincere about their craft and spend years studying. They would agree with the claim that it is impossible to believe that everyone born in September should 'expect financial success on Thursday'. 'Of course the tabloid stars are too vague to give specific direction. They are just general outlines of the aspects that are in sequence. For a more detailed prediction it is necessary to have an individual chart drawn up using the time and date of birth.'

Astrologers speak about their craft as though it were a science, yet astrology is not astronomy. That planets and stars are able to directly affect individual people's lives has never been scientifically proved. In essence, astrology is really a polytheistic religion. Without going into the full history of astrology, which would be far too enormous a subject for us to explore here (we recommend that you read Charles Strohmer's book, *What Your Horoscope Doesn't Tell You*[9]), modern astrology is based on Roman and Greek mythology.

In the lap of the gods

The horoscope shows that Saturn is moving into a particular sign. To the lay person this means that somewhere up there the planet Saturn is moving about, and on its travels it has come into the bit of the cosmos that is supposedly directly related to the day you happened to have been born. The horoscope goes on to describe the effect that this will have on your particular sign and therefore your life. (Obviously, the horoscope takes into account the position of other planets as well.) Saturn is said to affect people in a constricting, malevolent sort of a way, but surely Saturn is just a planet with a lot of rings around it?

What the astrologers are really describing is not the character and personality of an enormous lump of rocks and gases, but the character and personality of the mythical Roman god Saturn who was revered as a sinister and threatening primeval power.

Descriptions of Jupiter, Venus, Mars, Neptune and Pluto are all exactly the same as the descriptions of the gods of the Roman polytheistic age. Gods in the guise of planets are said to affect parts of the human anatomy, human behaviour and personality, and are even said to be able to govern the right time to plant particular vegetables for maximum flavour. Astrology, no matter how long it is studied, no matter how many case examples match up to or seem to verify its claims, is founded on a myth!

What a coincidence!

So how does it work? Well, obviously if a tabloid horoscope is read by millions of people, there are always going to be those who by sheer coincidence will meet a tall dark handsome stranger on Friday night. Laws of probability tell us that much. Astrology is addictive. Many people say that they only read it as a joke. 'I only read it last thing at night to see what kind of a day I've had!' Most of the time they forget what they have read—it doesn't fit, it means nothing to them. But every now and again a little spark of something that it says rings true and they are amazed. One accurate prediction can often speak higher than many vague and forgettable ones. 'I won't say I completely believe in it, but every now and again it's uncanny!'

But what about those individual predictions? Surely

that's not coincidence? Certainly, the charts that astrologers painstakingly draw up are often supernaturally accurate, but how? We have established that there is no proven evidence that planets can actually have power over individual lives, but this revelatory information must come from somewhere. The Bible is very clear that this sort of divination is not from God, so the only other explanation to the extraordinary insight that many astrologers have, outside of what they have studied, must come from spirit guides. Many astrologers would acknowledge that they are able to know things about their clients' past, present and future that they have no explanation for, other than that they must have become very skilled in their art and somehow be intuitive to these things. Others are more open in acknowledging supernatural guidance from channelled entities.

Star struck!

Astrologers claim that once an individual knows who they really are according to the stars, they can then make free decisions about their lives. It's amazing, however, what the power of suggestion can achieve. If someone is told that they are incompatible with anyone born under the sign Gemini, you can almost guarantee that once they discover their boss is a Gemini there will be tension in the office. Alternatively, when told that they are very suited to Taureans, they will immediately relax in their company and in doing so probably aid the relationship considerably. Perhaps for some, being told that because they were born in a particular month means that they will be confident and assertive is all the incentive they need to be just that. Predictions can bless, and they can curse!

Questions

Almost anything—bad behaviour, mood swings, nasty accidents, even the fact that you failed an exam (regardless of how much studying you did or didn't do)—can be put down to the position of the stars. Astrology cures all guilt. 'How can I be responsible for my actions, officer? The stars made me do it!' There are, however, a few questions which astrology has yet to answer.

Did you know that the rules that govern astrology were drawn up before people had even heard of or seen the planets Uranus, Neptune and Pluto? How then can they be accurate? Of course, their supposed influence over individual people's lives have now been taken into consideration, but does this mean that all those previous horoscopes are invalid? After all, the planets were there all the time. And what of the millions of stars and planets that we still don't know about?

Identical twins born only minutes apart can grow up to lead completely different lives. Surely a matter of minutes cannot make such a marked difference in the planetary influences that are exerted on them. What if two babies were born in the same hospital at exactly the same time—would they have identical lives?

Does it mean that above the Arctic circle, where there may be no planet in sight for several weeks so that it is almost impossible to calculate the zodiacal points, the people born there technically have no horoscope? Astrologically, they don't exist!

Plus, how is it that in tragedies such as earthquakes and train crashes, hundreds of people can die all at the same time? Surely, if an individual's birth chart dictates the planetary influence over their life, it will also govern their death? It cannot be overridden by any other planetary influence because it was determined at birth and must run its course.

Problem

The problem is that astrology is not just a harmless side-line, not just a spiritual lift—it is a religion. The advice that it hands out might not demand that people alter their moral stance: it might not demand anything at all, except that you believe in mythological gods disguised as planets. Many people have found themselves drawn further into occult practices through their 'harmless' dabblings with astrology, living in fear of its superstitious predictions and unable to take independent control of their lives. It is dangerous to seek fulfilment and purpose in a myth, and suicide to be guided by it to make important life decisions (Is 47:12–15).

Astrology is the basis on which the New Age is founded. The idea that a New Age is dawning is based on the belief that the whole world has been in the age of Pisces and according to the zodiac cycle is due to move into the age of Aquarius. But if astrology is a myth, where does that leave the New Age?

7

Politics, Power and the Planet

In the sixties, the hippies were the counter-culture's political radicals, campaigning on the streets, staging sit-ins and walk-outs, and even staying in bed just to make their point. In the new radical techno-nineties it's the turn of the zippies to enter the world stage and challenge the political scene.

According to EPI, the *Encyclopaedia Psychedelia International* (New Age magazine for the switched on and tuned in), the technoperson 'understands that rationality, organisation, long-term planning, consistency and single-mindedness are necessary to achieve anything on the material plane'. A hippy, however, 'understands that vision, individuality, spontaneity, flexibility and open-mindedness are crucial to realise anything on the spiritual plane'. Put these two together and you have a 'zippy' (techno-nineties hippy), or 'Zen-inspired professional pagan'.

As you turn to the first page of EPI, you are warned to be prepared to 'encounter something beyond style which aims to create a consciousness-craze that will save the planet'. Saving the planet is foremost in the minds of the majority of New Agers, and it is for this reason that the New Age worldview is being presented to the voter on the street by today's political radicals who have decided to nail their colours to the mast. Here today, green tomorrow.

The paradox

On the surface, New Agers seem to be saying that it's okay for people to believe anything they like. After all, why should anyone have the right to tell someone else exactly what to believe? If there is no absolute truth, it's unreasonable to expect others to agree completely with your viewpoint. This is why there is so much diversity of thinking within the New Age, and why it's so difficult to put your finger successfully on what it is and where it is. There are no headquarters, and there is no official manifesto. Or is there?

You may create your own reality, and you are perfectly entitled to be into whatever form of paranormal experience you so wish, and, indeed, call it what you like, so long as you understand the basics, the underlying worldview that all is part of the same oneness. People are allowed to be individuals so long as their individuality doesn't detract from the foundational message that all is interconnected, interdependent and ultimately unable to be separated.

The message of a coming New Age has been shouted from the rooftops. Little by little, the age of Aquarius notion has infiltrated society, through the media, through medicine, through networks of people exchanging ideas and techniques to bring east to west more effectively. But there is only one way really to get things done, only one way really to affect the very heart of the nation and to shake the world, and that is to infiltrate the political scene.

New Age politics

Telling the general public that they need to change their life and their thinking about the world and reality, and expecting them to be able to manage that change effectively while they are directed by a governmental system based in 'the old way of thinking', is impossible. A world dominated by a system which promotes material profitability above all moral, ethical and spiritual issues, will never endorse the Aquarian lifestyle that New Agers believe is essential for the evolutionary progression of mankind. The aim of the New Age political radical is to form a coalition between politics and spirituality, uniting the two to pave the way for a New Age.

Not everybody is a political animal. To many, their vote is determined by the way they were brought up: 'We always vote this way. My father voted the same as me.' They really cannot tell you the motivation behind their cross in the box. The more cynical and disillusioned electorate are convinced that it's all a matter of 'swings and roundabouts'. The party promises the earth, and then, when they are in power, they are really no better than the last lot. The difference is that the problems have been shifted slightly. The fact that many have become disillusioned with traditional political solutions is reflected in the increasing number of votes registered for the radical liberal parties who until recently made no impact on the political world stage. Screaming Lord Sutch of the Monster Raving Loony Party is a regular contender for the 'I haven't got a clue who to vote for, and anyway, what difference does my vote make to the price of butter?' vote. The time has come for a new option.

Sign of the times

Events of the past few years or so have been staggering. It was a sobering moment indeed when we realised that the Iron Curtain, that for so long overshadowed world politics, keeping the superpowers of the United States and the Soviet Union separate, was crumbling. The Berlin Wall has now been dismantled and sold off in small chunks to tourists keen to take home a piece of living history. East Germans have now become integrated into the west. Ceaucescu was executed, and Romania was liberated from the despotic regime under which it had been oppressed, only to be faced by new problems. Glasnost and Perestroika heralded the end of Soviet communism. The cold war is now well and truly over, and daily there is more news of a continuing liberation spurred by a people no longer content with their lot.

It's a small world. Modern transport and communication have promoted a 'world vision'. Years ago, people would only have travelled abroad if they were extremely adventurous, exploring types, or if they were forced to go because of war, work or circumstances beyond their control. Now it is the social and acceptable norm for people to spend most of their bank holidays camping in airport lounges, waiting for the flight to their annual fortnight package holiday destination. Maureen Lipman is promoting cheap rate phone calls to relatives in Australia, while our television screens are full of programmes filmed all over the globe. Even if you never leave the comfort of your armchair, you can flit around the world at the touch of your TV 'zapper', exploring the heart of the Amazon jungle, climbing to the summits of the world's mountain ranges and learning about the cultural idiosyncrasies of tribal natives.

People are more able to identify with the problems of different nations, regardless of the distance between them in terms of miles, cultural differences and language barriers. This is reflected in the large amounts of money collected as people put their hands in their pockets to contribute to the fund-raising activities of the growing number of emergency groups that provide aid for the many world disaster zones.

Growing unity

This growing unity is good news for all of us. For too long the world has been divided, with countries clinging to national boundaries with patriotic fervour, terrified of being overrun, unable to trust, to work together, to share resources. There is always the threat of war, and the more well balanced of us are convinced that war is not a good thing. World peace is top on the list of things that most people would like to see in their lifetime. This century, however, has seen more than its fair share of warfare, more than its fair share of death, as a result of individual greed.

For the New Age radical, growing unity between nations, between people groups, is not only essential to promote world peace, but inevitable. The inevitable outcome of the coming New Age is that as people come to realise that all is one they will also realise that there is basically no difference between themselves and others. We are all interconnected; we are all one.

To New Agers, patriotism and nationalism are the result of a false consciousness from the old age that promoted the idea of separateness and ·exclusivity, and they are keen to encourage that this type of thinking be transcended. New Age politics is global politics. It is not enough to consider oneself a citizen of one country; each person must develop a global perspective and recognise that they are connected to the whole, a planetary citizen. New Age politics must reflect New Age spirituality. If all is one, then people must behave as one, and in the words of John Lennon from his song 'Imagine': 'The world will be as one!'

Planetary perspectives

The problem is that New Agers also recognise that it is essential to their thinking that in uniting the world and promoting planetary consciousness no harm should come to any individual group's cultural heritage. So there is a measure of controversy and conflict between New Agers and their more radical political fringe who demand a new world order.

Planetary Citizens is a group dedicated to transforming the world through political action. Founded in 1973 by Donald Keys, a consultant to the United Nations delegations and committees for many years, its members include David Spangler and Peter Caddy of the Findhorn community in northern Scotland. It was Keys who put forward the idea that the United Nations, although in itself not a New Age organisation, could be 'the nexus of emerging planetary consciousness'.[10]

When the United Nations was formed after the Second World War, its primary aim was to promote world peace. Instrumental in bringing together otherwise individualistic nations, the UN has become a force to be reckoned with, involving itself more and more in issues of global well-being, from famine aid to regulating education programmes in third world countries.

World government

Ultimately, what most New Age political activists would advocate is a world government: one body with representatives of all tribes and nations having their say in regulating and controlling the events which shape the planet. A new economic order in which all resources are shared equally across the globe would then be implemented, alongside a global taxation system. In this vision of one world there would be no need for armaments, because everything would be collectively owned and all would be one. Unifying economic, political and social issues to one world government would be very difficult to implement practically, so the majority of New Age political activists would suggest that this would be best done through a system of civil government decentralisation, in which the specific directives of the central body over socio-economic issues are applied to the local area in more practical, hands-on ways.

The one world utopian system is not a new idea. Marilyn Ferguson, in her book *The Aquarian Conspiracy*,[11] gave the credit for the idea to Pierre Teilhard de Chardin who died in 1955. A Jesuit paleontologist and philosopher, he predicted the 'planetisation of mankind', outlining that there would come a time when new people with a planetary perspective and an inclusive awareness of life would identify instinctively with the entire human species and all of planetary life. Teilhard de Chardin called this state of one world consciousness 'omega', and it is to this omega that many New Age activists look. They would say that it is closer than we think as people begin to move from egocentricity to a shared awareness of planetary problems.

New Transformationalist politicians are those New Age political activists who believe that both individually and corporately, we need to be transformed in our thinking and in our subsequent actions. This is tied in with their belief that we are on the verge of a quantum leap necessary to bring mankind and all the cosmos into the new age of Aquarius. They combine issues such as feminism, environmentalism, the human potential movement, modern technology and a more simple, less material lifestyle, and weave them into a New Age worldview in which the idea that everything is one is an inherent part. Holistic politics are the agenda for social transformation, which involves the creation of an interrelated system wherein all the issues and all of the problems of people and the planet are dealt with as a whole. In this way, the politicians hope to be able to combat the perceived negativity of past systems which treated the earth, the state and humanity as separate and isolated entities.

Economics

Traditional economists have been criticised, not just because profit has always been the overriding factor in their decision making, but also that they have been guilty of a very fragmented approach, failing to recognise that the economy, ecology and sociology are intertwined. The economists have always looked to theoretical models of economic growth in order to plan and strategise. However, the past has shown us that in practice this has led to major problems, including: the growing population; increasing food shortage in some countries, while others have vast food mountains that they cannot get rid of; and vast dust bowls brought about as plains are cleared for increasing numbers of cattle to be grazed to match consumer demand for meat. All these examples are living proof that sometimes man does not know best. Many would say that we need to adopt a systems-based thinking for our economics and that this systems thinking is of primary importance to our planetary survival.

A system of systems

The earth is covered with a networking pattern of ecosystems. These ecosystems are designed to be self-balancing. Everything we do has a knock-on effect. Just by being, we cannot fail to challenge, change and catalyse the world around us. No matter how conscious we are of using the resources around us, we still make waste. We breathe in oxygen and breathe out carbon dioxide, a waste product. Thankfully, the world has been designed to cope with this and plants take in CO_2 and give out oxygen. So as long as we have plant life, we're laughing, or breathing—whichever way you like to look at it. But the fact of the matter is that we do affect our environment, positively or negatively.

In Arizona, scientists have initiated another of their ambitious Biosphere projects to find ways in which the world can be self-sufficient without damage to the environment. The idea is that in a defined area, hermetically sealed from the outside world, an artificial planet is created under glass. Inside, there is a smaller version of every major ecosystem, with examples of most of the major plant groups, some animals carefully selected to maintain the balance of the food chain, and six human beings. They are all locked inside this world within the world for two years and, hopefully, they will cope. To New Agers this hermetically sealed 'bubble world' represents more than just an experiment in effective resource management; it represents their own theory that this biosphere—the one that you are now sitting on—is really just a macro version of the micro one in Arizona. There is no outside input (no God figure)—just everything taking an active part in the cycle of life, each thing affecting something else because it is interrelating.

For the New Age activist, it is not enough to ask people to comply with a systems approach when applying economic strategy. It is essential that there is also a global acceptance of the mystical roots of this system theory, that all is interconnected, all is interdependent, because all is one. It does not occur to the New Age mind that this system of systems— the way the world has been designed to balance itself and work effectively of its own accord—could be the work of a master craftsman. To the New Ager it is only evidence that all is energy, constantly moving and rebalancing, shifting and changing, never being destroyed, just switching identity from time to time.

The New Age view is that because all is interconnected, because everything is essentially the same, we should, in theory, be able to identify with everybody else's predicament. You might not be experiencing for yourself what someone else is going through, but, in a more cosmic, spiritual sense, the New Ager would say that you are. It's all part of being interconnected. For this reason, they say, there should be no restraints put on people; we are all in the same boat, all experiencing the same situations, even though we may not be aware of it. Therefore, New Agers advocate a complete turnabout of policy over political issues that govern individual liberties, with a loosening of the restrictions. Since all are believed to be like God, able to create their own truth, why should anyone be able to tell people what they should or shouldn't be allowed to do? New Agers would say that such restrictions are self-limiting since we are all interconnected.

However, logic insists that without order, chaos reigns, and New Age politicians are as aware of this fact as any other. Take, for example, the issues of contraception and abortion—emotive and personal subjects. On the one hand, the New Age view would be that since the individual has freedom of choice over all issues of morality, no one should have authority to insist what individuals should or shouldn't choose regarding their family, or indeed their unborn child. On the other hand, economics insist that since the earth is increasingly overpopulated and resources are stretched beyond our capacity to cope, ultimately the answer will entail the curbing of the population.

Ideally, everyone should be able to do whatever they choose, but the consequences of such individual liberty are ultimately restrictive to the global population. The paradox is that the New Age political activists will inevitably have to insist on policies that contradict their philosophy.

Global chaos

The paradox is that if they really do live up to their principle that we are all God and therefore create our own reality; if they really allowed people to have that kind of moral freedom with no absolutes, no restrictions and no guidelines, there would be global chaos and social disorder on a grand scale. There has to be laws, there has to be guidelines, there has to be a moral framework, and it is this framework that gives liberty and security and not the anarchic utopian system that New Agers are keen to advocate. It just wouldn't work!

So far, New Age politicians have not substantially affected the political climate. There is much talk, but little real action. They do not have the power they require to establish this new world order. However, New Age groups have had some success in affecting the way that the public thinks and that is in the area of the environment.

Are you ozone friendly?

On the eastern shores of the Gulf, the sinister black water oozed its way onto the shore as ITN filmed the horrifying results of Saddam Hussein's plot to sabotage the Kuwait oil fields. Hundreds of cormorants covered in oil choked for breath, and the livelihood of the people in the coastal towns was threatened as they realised that there would be nothing left alive in the waters.

Years ago, the average child in the classroom could not have told you what or where the ozone layer is. Now, thanks to the publicity of the many environmentalist groups, the issue of pollution and impending environmental disaster has become front page news. CFCs—chloro-fluro-carbons—have been removed from most major brands of toiletries and cleaning products, and supermarkets are now proud to present recycled, ozone friendly, biodegradable products on their shelves, knowing that the market for these goods has soared sky high.

For too long the general public has been unaware that the result of our material consumer society has been that the planet has suffered. Acid rain, the greenhouse effect, disappearing forestland, and other issues have been brought to the public eye, and not soon enough. Thankfully, people are now beginning to realise that there is a price to pay and we must be responsible in the use of our resources. The Bible tells us that in the beginning God gave man dominion over all the earth, with a specific mandate to look after it and steward it wisely. Sadly, this mandate has been neglected. Dominion has been misinterpreted as domination, never part of the plan of God whose ideal for human leadership and authority is that of a servant, serving all that we have been placed in charge of. More evidence to suggest that it would have been wise to have listened to God all along instead of learning the hard way, usually when it's too late (as in the case of the dodo).

The green issue is one that deserves considerable attention—far more than we can possibly devote here. If there is anything that we can learn from the message of the New Age, it is that we need to pay more attention to what we are doing to the planet. Far too many of us have been so busy feathering our own nests that we have not considered the irreparable devastation of our environment. Christians—and we hold up our hands as guilty—are just as much to blame, spending so much of our time trying to save each other and not enough time saving the things we have been given to look after. It is as well that this issue has been so widely publicised. Something desperately needs to be done, and environmental issues present to us in the nineties a challenge which we dare not ignore.

How far do we go?

If we are to meet the challenge that the environmental issue is facing us with, we need to be careful to approach it wisely. Wildly joining in with any group or activity which claims that it will 'save the planet' is not necessarily the best move.

A friend of ours innocently wrote for more information from the organisation Friends of the Earth and was very surprised to receive back not only the information she wanted on the environment, but also endorsements for New Age workshops on psychic healing and information about New Age therapeutic music. Friends of the Earth may not themselves have a cast iron New Age agenda—unlike Greenpeace, whose flagship, The Rainbow Warrior, was named after a shamanistic prophecy—but they are clearly not adverse to promoting these alternatives to prospective greens, as if it were an inherent part of the package.

Jonathan Porritt, who has become a leading voice of the environmental issue, claims that in his quest to help to rebalance the current crisis, he has found himself spiritually linked with the earth itself. Interviewed in *Q* magazine, he explained that although he no longer hugs as many trees as he used to, he cannot deny that there is 'a real mystical, spiritual link with the earth' which drives him to be more than concerned about what we are doing to the planet.

We need to be aware of the ethos behind the various organisations that are actively affecting our world. On the one hand, it is very good that their projects are actively making a difference to the environment, but on the other it is disturbing that in promoting a green approach to life they are also advocating a New Age worldview, even as far as James Lovelock's Gaia approach—the earth as God.

Clearly, we must look after the planet and manage its resources, but we need to do that with a clear understanding that the earth and everything in it is created and is not God. We must be careful not to exploit animals, using cruelty and inhumane practice, but we need to remember from a biblical perspective that, lovely though animals are, in the created order they are not on the same level as human beings. Therefore, we need to be wary of groups who would advocate violent and aggressive measures against other people in order to promote their way of thinking. For example, the Animal Liberation Front with their extremist approach, issuing 'eye for an eye' attacks on those conducting research that involves animal experimentation. Also, some branches of the Hunt Saboteur movement that would actively support using violence against hunters in order to prevent hunts from taking place.

Let's not throw the baby out with the bathwater by shoving the green issue under the carpet, or worse, labelling the whole area as New Age and therefore somehow weird. The environment is not a New Age issue. Being green does not necessarily mean being

New Age. The global situation is a global problem. Eventually, it will affect all of us in one way or another, and so it is up to us to approach the subject seriously. The green slogan is very apt for the way that we should be living our lives today: 'Think globally, act locally, respond personally.' It really is going to take this kind of personal commitment to make a difference to the state of the planet.

Our advice would be that before joining any organisation or party (and this also applies outside the green issue) you should research its way of thinking. If the group promotes a New Age perspective in terms of interconnectedness (all is one, as we have explained in previous chapters), or if the organisation encourages members, either during a conference, seminar or through its literature, to adopt any form of New Age technique to promote oneness (such as attuning, yogic meditation and visualisation) you should be very wary about your involvement.

The world in union

Kiri Te Kanawa sang the theme for the 1991 Rugby World Cup to the tune of 'I vow to thee my country'. A rousing, almost spiritual song, titled 'The World in Union', its link with Rugby Union was very clear. It was a song about taking part, being together, putting aside political issues and playing a game of sport together.

It is wonderful that in sport nations can come together, and everyone would love to see the day when we put aside prejudices and bitter quarrels over land and enjoy peace. After all, it was the apostle Paul who, in his letter to the Roman church, explained that in the kingdom of God there is no difference between people. Whatever colour they are, whatever nationality, whatever their position in society, in God's eyes they are the same.

The trouble is that within this song there is the line, 'As we climb to meet our destiny, a new age has begun.' Let's not jump off at the deep end. Certainly, the term 'new age' is used by many to mean a new time, the next chapter in history, and it does not have the east/west spiritual mishmash connotations that the New Age has. But what is all this stuff about meeting our destiny? Are we as human beings on the verge of a new look, a new way of life on this planet? Are we destined to step into a new evolutionary phase—to take on the mantle of Aquarian man?

From apes to Adam

The theory of evolution is a major part of New Age ideology. The age of Aquarius is supposedly the next step in the evolutionary ladder for human beings, but of course there is no proof of this.

In recognising the world as a system of energy that is constantly flowing from one order to the next, it is believed that this energy is, over time, able to reconstruct itself or emerge to become the most effective form or forms necessary for survival. It is supposed that the cosmic consciousness, this universal energy, is a self-organising dynamic force and that it is able to evolve selectively. This would indicate that the evolutionary process is not random but purposeful and creative.

The Darwinian theory of evolution has never been conclusively proved since there have been no valid findings of the remains of those in the half and half transition between ape and man. The missing link is still missing. Darwin's theory of natural selection and subsequent evolutionary change had no spiritual base, giving no hope for the future of the planet or of the individual. Yet New Agers attribute much hope to their brand of emergent evolution, in which the collective consciousness is able to organise itself into structures and forms far greater than the original, far beyond the sum of the parts. To the New Ager, two plus two is very definitely twelve when the one takes a quantum evolutionary leap.

Evolutionists, sobered by the fact that there is little real proof of the transitionary stages of evolution, have come to the conclusion that little real change occurs while the specimen is alive, but that new species just appear, evolving all at once, completely formed. This radical punctuated evolution is supposedly caused as extra stress is placed on the species or even the planet as a whole and all of a sudden there is a radical change. One day dinosaurs; the next, herds of cows grazing in the pasture.

Evolution—the New Age hope

Evolution is inseparable from New Age concepts of God, of man, of history, of salvation, and of spiritual growth. In essence, evolution is the mainstay of the New Age philosophy. Without evolution there would be no Aquarian age and there would be no hope that people would become spiritually and mystically aware of oneness with the one. Without evolution, the one wouldn't be the one because it would not be able to encapsulate all that is and nothing would have been formed out of the energy that is called the one. Evolution is New Agers' hope, and they believe that it is only a paradigm shift, a massive evolutionary leap, that will change the world.

But how can New Agers be certain that evolution is advancing humanity? So far, if the collective consciousness, or the one, is so clever, it's been hiding its light well and truly under a bushel because the world is in a catastrophic mess. Technology has brought us to a crisis point in overpopulation, unemployment, famine, depleting and wasted resources, the nuclear threat, war, poverty and environmental collapse. If nothing else, the gruesome realities of today's world are enough to undermine belief in an evolutionary process. The New Age belief that all of a sudden a New Age will dawn and the world will be turned about because the one has shifted in emphasis, requires incredible faith.

Christian citizenship

So how do we approach the very real issues of today's world, without going down the New Age path? As we have already stressed from a Christian and biblical worldview, we need to recognise that every one of us has a responsibility to care for the world around us. We have been given the task of managing world resources and of ensuring that all people groups are cared for in the same way that we would care for ourselves. Jesus made it very clear that the greatest of the commandments is that we should love one another (Jn 13:34).

We need to be aware that as Christians we are called to be witnesses of the truth about Jesus Christ, and that we are to do this through verbally preaching the gospel of the kingdom of God, and by demonstrating through our lifestyle what it is to be a follower of Jesus and showing what being a part of God's kingdom really involves. We are to be salt and light in the community in which we live (Mt 5:13), and that means we must be active. It has been said that as Christians, 'we have a belief that behaves'.[12] It is what we do when we think that no one is looking that reflects what we really believe and where we are at.

As Christians, we are citizens not only of the country in which we live, but also of God's kingdom. We are Christian citizens. Citizenship is a real buzz word for the 1990s, carrying a sense that we all have rights and responsibilities.

We do believe that we need to unite if we really are to affect what is going on in the world, but not in the sense that New Agers would advocate. It is about time that the Christian church united around the issue that Jesus Christ is really good news, bringing hope and release to everyone, and this should be demonstrated to all nations through words and deeds.

At times this will mean that we will have to work alongside those whom we don't necessarily agree with on all points, but it is essential that we are able to be co-belligerents when facing particular issues. Let us make the important issues our common enemy and work together to see them overcome.

As Christians, we believe that God is a creative God who wants his creation to advance with people expressing their individuality in different ways, taking responsibility for their lives.

The Bible reveals that God identifies particularly with the poor, oppressed and socially marginalised.

In the Old Testament, God measured Israel's heart and righteousness by whether or not they were caring for 'the alien . . . the fatherless and the widow' in their midst (Ps 146:9; see also Is 1:17; Jas 1:27).

We believe that, as Christian citizens, we must live a life of self-sacrifice, but we need not and should not give up everything that is good or enjoyable. Christians should not condemn anything which God himself does not condemn, but we should stand against attitudes which God hates. These include racism, sexism, nationalism, materialism, idolatry and all oppression of minorities. We should give ourselves to those who are ill-treated and to empowering the powerless, following the model of Jesus' life.

Jesus was incredibly radical, both in the things that he said and in the way that he lived out his life. The first person that he revealed his identity as Messiah to was a woman, and a Samaritan at that (two incredibly oppressed groups of people at that time). Jesus crossed cultural barriers and stirred up those in authority, not in an anarchic sense because he was keen to demonstrate that we are to be lawful under the authority of those who have been commissioned to govern, but in order that the truth of God could be demonstrated.

The kingdom of God is one of justice, reconciliation and peace. The good news about Jesus is that it is possible by God's grace for wrongs to be righted, for people to be reconciled with God, and to live in peace, secure and whole. Salvation is about being whole, having our wholeness restored to us.

The personal living God is calling together a people who, in relationship with him through his Son Jesus Christ, and empowered by the Holy Spirit, are willing

to live out the Great Commission that Jesus outlined
to his disciples in Matthew 28:18–20: to preach the
full gospel of the kingdom to all nations and all people
groups, demonstrating it in our words and in our lifestyle to bring reconciliation and wholeness to the
people, and to the planet. It is a challenge that we
really cannot ignore.

8

The Choice

A true life story (continued)

She knew that she had reached the end of the line.
One way or another she would have to find a way to
get out of this mess. What was it that had prompted
her in her hour of need to call on Jesus, of all people?
'Gentle Jesus, meek and mild.' She'd been taught as
a child to say her prayers every night before she went
to sleep, but surely Jesus was just a myth, a fairy tale
that adults grew out of. The Christians that she had
known were all wimps—namby-pamby people with
tambourines and awful haircuts, and hardly a people
of power. She needed to get out of London. Perhaps
that was the answer. She would simply ignore the
events of the last few days, blocking them out of her
mind by sheer force of will. She would ignore the
telepathic link that she had with a friend called
Simon—ignore his pleading voice. She would visit her
cousin in Chichester to try to relax to get some
perspective on matters. Remember, you are special,
you can overcome anything, she told herself.

Confused and frightened, she got on the train.
Frightened, because she was almost certain that she
was to meet her fate in Chichester. On previous

occasions when her cousin had invited her to stay, Samuel had categorically warned her against it. 'You will die in Chichester,' he had told her, and so she had cancelled, pretending to be too busy to go. Now she was on the train, travelling towards the south coast, but travelling to what? Tears rolled down her face as she quietly repeated the words of the Lord's prayer over and over again. If Jesus is just a myth or if he was only just a good teacher, if all there is in the spiritual realm is a series of feuding spirits some more powerful than others, if human beings are all there is, if I am supposed to have the power to overcome everything, there is no hope!

Her cousin welcomed her at the station, and meekly she got into the car. The weekend went by very quickly. the soon relaxed in the company of her cousin and the friends that she had met in Chichester. The interesting thing was that all those whom she met were Christians; at least, that was how they described themselves to her. Once, she had chatted at length to a guy who told her that he had a personal relationship with God, not a spirit being and not his alter ego, but the Creator of the universe. She was intrigued.

On the Sunday she agreed to go to church to 'check it out'. Surprisingly, all the people inside were enjoying themselves. There was an atmosphere of fun and friendship, and she felt very at ease with the surroundings and all that was going on—a far cry from her childhood experiences of church as a cold, uninviting place where everyone was silent and guilty. A guy stood up at the front and introduced himself as the leader of the church. He was young, with blond spiky hair and dressed in blue jeans; not at all what she had expected. He began his talk.

'You may remember that thirteen weeks ago I was going to do a talk, but I lost my notes at the last minute. Well, it just so happens that on Friday night at around 6 pm I found them. So today I am going to be speaking on the subject of the occult: ouija boards, spiritism, and all of that kind of thing.'

She couldn't believe it. The time that he had lost the notes had been the weekend that she had cancelled coming to Chichester, and he'd found them again at the time that she'd pulled into Chichester on the train. It was as if this guy knew everything about what she'd been into. She felt almost as if the talk had been written specifically about her. He explained about truth, about God and about Satan, and he used the Bible to expose the occult and its spirits as pathological liars. As she listened to what he said, the truth became evident to her; the truth was to be found in Jesus.

At the end of his talk, he invited anyone who had been involved in contacting spirits or any of the forms of occult practice, to come to the side of the hall if they wanted to talk more or be prayed for. She stood bolt upright and pushed past her very surprised cousin. She walked over to where there were a few people from the church ready to talk and to pray, and with as much courage as she could muster and shaking like a leaf, she said, 'My name is Andrea, and I want nothing to stand between me and God any more.'

'Bible bashers'

Christians are often given bad press. They always have something to say on any given subject, and it's usually negative, a real downer to whatever is going on in society. They are caricatured as boring, repressive, old-fashioned 'Bible bashers' who are definitely not good news. The New Age, on the other hand, is marketed as the up-to-the-minute happening scene, where everything and anything goes. From the outside it would appear to be the answer to any fears of repression. So how come the New Age is so inclusive and Christianity so exclusive? Why won't the two mix?

We have already seen that the New Ager would say that Christians are trapped in old age thinking. To those with a Christian or biblical view, the story is very different. They would say that the New Age is merely the result of an old age lie or heresy that has taken on a New Age disguise.

The Bible is often slated as being inaccurate or full of contradictions by those who really have no grounds to comment. As a matter of fact, there is so much archaeological evidence and historical documentation that proves its accuracy that we are able to hold it up as a reliable Scripture. Why not get yourself a copy and see for yourself that it really isn't the stuffy old book its critics make it out to be? In fact, it has a lot of relevant things to say. (Not a lot of people know that!) Try to look up the references that we give you, and see for yourself. We're not just making it up as we go along.

The lie and the Fall

However you might interpret the first book of the Bible, the basic story of mankind's downfall is quite clear to see. The one thing that Adam and Eve were told not to do was eat from the tree of the knowledge of good and evil. In order to live in obedience to God, who had given them free will, they were to obey that one command. Satan, jealous of God, angry and full of hatred for God's most prized creation, sold them this line: 'You can be like God.' What better way to tempt the ego than to be convinced that you too could be God, all powerful, the creator of all that is, of all reality? Hooked on this line, mankind disobeyed God, turning to its own devices. And so Adam and Eve became separated from their Creator, more and more convinced that they could go it alone.

The lie that mankind was sold right at the very beginning is the same as that which the New Age is marketing today. And, as we have already discovered, some, like Shirley Maclaine, would go as far as chanting, 'I am God' as part of their daily worship.

So what are Christians saying today to combat the New Age? If they are so convinced that it is not the truth, what is? Is there any good news?

Now for the good news

The biblical worldview, as we have seen, is quite literally worlds away from that of the New Ager, and it is centred on one fact: that God, the personal, knowable, creator of everything, wants to have an exciting, dynamic, supernatural, liberating relationship with every single person, man, woman and child, and that he has made this possible. The Christian message, or the gospel, really is good news.

The word 'gospel' was used in the ancient Greek world as a term for a message of victory. It was an announcement of great news and joy. The Christian message of the New Testament is a proclamation of the greatest victory the world has ever known (1 Cor 15:57). To many, the Christian message sounds weak, far too simple to be true. Many would rather believe that the truth, if there is only one truth, is complicated, to be studied at length and with great perseverance, and that only the most determined and intellectual will really understand it. But the Bible tells us that the gospel is the power of God, and although it may seem foolish to some it is the only way to salvation (1 Cor 1:18; Rom 1:16). God has made himself accessible to everyone, no matter what their IQ might be.

The difference between the message of the Bible and that of the New Age, is that God, separate from his creation, has made a move actively to intervene in our lives. It is not us striving to be something, striving to understand, striving for enlightenment, but rather the good news is that God has made the first move. Understanding our predicament, God so desperately wants to offer his grace to us that he has provided a way for us to make up for our disobedience to him so that our relationship can be reconciled. The good news is that God wants to bless us with a fulfilling, satisfying life, free from guilt and secure in the knowledge that we are at peace with God and have a secure eternal future.

And the good news is about a person. Not a set of beliefs, not a complex philosophy or a set of moral rules and regulations to live by, but about a real historical figure. Not just a man, but also God.

All throughout the Bible, the message of God's intervention in human history leads to the dramatic entrance of Jesus onto the world stage. People are often surprised to discover that Jesus is indeed a real person. Many would accept that Julius Caesar was breathing and walking around on the earth, yet they consider Jesus as some kind of fairy tale character. The truth is that there is more documented evidence for the existence of Jesus than there is for Julius Caesar. But how could one person be good news?

The truth and the consequences

There have been many important men and women in history who are known for the contribution that they made to the lives of particular groups of people living in certain parts of the world. Jesus was a man who in his life and death affected the lives of all peoples in all nations for all time. But how?

God, the source of all life (not the life-force of the New Ager but, as we have outlined, a personal God with a distinct character and personality) created men and women in his image in order that they could have a friendship relationship with him. There is no sense in having a friendship with someone who has no choice about being your friend. The beauty of all real friendship and all real love is that the two parties are able actively to choose it. God gave humanity free will for this purpose. He had to present guidelines to us in order that this choice could be actively used, and so God made it possible for us to choose to obey him. But people go their own way. Humanity went its own way and disobeyed God.

Sin is a word that is very much out of vogue, but it's really an ancient archery term. When the archer's arrow missed the target, it was said that they had sinned, fallen short of the mark, and so they would have to aim their sights higher. The Bible tells us that 'all have sinned and fall short of the glory of God' (Rom 3:23). The problem is that every single one of us is guilty of missing the mark in our lives. We may not be any better or any worse than anybody else, but the truth is that we have thought and said and done things that we know are wrong and certainly don't match up to the mark of perfection. All of us at one time or another have gone away from the maker's instructions for how we should live our lives, and that really is a problem because it means quite simply that we have been disobedient to God.

If we as individuals choose to turn away from God, what we are actively doing is walking away from life and towards death. The ultimate consequence for our disobedience is complete separation from God— complete separation from life itself. Jesus said that he came to give us life and life to the full (Jn 10:10). God began his plan to reconcile himself with people by offering them the chance to live by rules and regulations, which was the law of the Old Testament. But time and time again, people proved that they could not live under the law. It was too restricting, too difficult to do, because they were constantly hampered by temptation. Humanity is unable to keep the law in its own strength. Knowing this to be the case, God, throughout the Old Testament, pointed to his plan to reconcile mankind to himself and make the ultimate sacrifice in order to rescue his people from the disaster of their separation from him. His plan was to send Jesus.

Because God has a distinct character and personality, and because he is the ultimate perfect truth, he is completely consistent. God is totally loving and merciful, but he is also completely just. If God were simply to overlook the things that we have done wrong, then he would not be just, and at the same time, if God punished everything that we have done without offering his hand to us, he would be cruel and heartless. Instead, God sent his only Son—fully man and fully God, the only person who didn't have a price on his own head because he never sinned—to pay the price for everyone with his own life.

Jesus lived a very ordinary life, and was tempted in every way that it is possible to be tempted, in order that he could prove that he had overcome sin. Then he went to his death freely, identifying completely with human suffering, in order that he could become the way in which mankind could be reconciled to God the Father.

Jesus was crucified, dying a horrific death, and then three days later he rose from the grave as a sign from God that for all time and for all those that choose it Jesus has finally sealed the victory over the power of sin (which separates us from God) and over death itself. The grave could not keep him down, and more than five hundred people witnessed him alive after his Resurrection (1 Cor 15:6).

Kingdoms in conflict

The good news is centred around a kingdom. A kingdom of justice and peace in which Jesus is the King. A kingdom that offers hope and liberation to all people groups, life and health, truth and reality, healing, wholeness and eternal salvation. The Bible tells us that there are two kingdoms: the kingdom of God and the kingdom of Satan. Satan is an angelic being who disobeyed God, becoming jealous and proud and finally being thrown out of God's presence. This evil being is described as one who is completely without hope, the father of all lies, the deceiver. Since there are only two kingdoms, the Bible is clear that you are either in one camp or the other—there is no middle ground. The kingdoms are in conflict, as different from one another as light and dark. The good news is that everyone can buy into the kingdom of God and all of its blessings by accepting God on his terms, and his terms are Jesus.

During Jesus' life on earth, he was good news to those around him. He performed many miracles, giving sight to the blind, healing the lame and bringing freedom to all those who were captive to their circumstances and under the power of Satan (Lk 4:16–21; Acts 10:38). Two thousand years later, Jesus is still good news because he is alive. God is alive and he wants to get involved!

The choice

To New Agers, personal transformation comes about only as a result of individuals employing some technique to change the way they think and react. A slow and arduous process of self-brainwashing, it is a mixture of becoming completely self-centred, believing that you are God, and at the same time denying that you have any individual self-worth because we are all interconnected we are all part of the same cosmic energy.

To Christians, personal transformation comes about only as they acknowledge that as unique individuals, with separate and distinct characters and personalities, they have a responsibility for their actions and the consequences of their self-will. A responsibility before God. Jesus said, 'I tell you the truth, no-one can see the kingdom of God unless he is born again' (Jn 3:3). He wasn't talking about reincarnation. He wasn't advocating employing some New Age rebirthing technique. He was calling people to follow him as the way back to God the Father. Because of Jesus, we can start again with a clean slate, free from the guilt of the things that we have done in the past. We are spiritually reborn. 'Therefore, if anyone is in Christ, he is a new creation; the old has gone, the new has come!' (2 Cor 5:17).

So how do we accept Jesus as the answer to our individual situations? The Bible says it's simple and it's very complicated.

Simply, it takes an individual admitting that he or she has messed things up by doing things that don't match up to God, by sinning. It then takes believing in Jesus, believing that he is the Son of God, believing that he died on the cross and rose from the dead in order that our sins could be forgiven and we could be reconciled with God. 'For it is by grace you have been saved, through faith—and this not from your-selves, it is the gift of God—not by works, so that no-one can boast' (Eph 2:8–9).

But knowing that you have done wrong and believing intellectually what Jesus did is not enough. We have a free choice—what will we do with it?

> If you confess with your mouth, 'Jesus is Lord,' and believe in your heart that God raised him from the dead, you will be saved. For it is with your heart that you believe and are justified, and it is with your mouth that you confess and are saved (Rom 10:9).

To repent is to make a complete 180-degree turn-around from what you are doing, completely sorry for what you have done and determined not to do it again. Jesus called people to follow him, and following is an active step. The fishermen who knew Jesus gave up everything they had when he called them to follow him. Even today, Jesus is extending an invitation to all those who will follow him, but following means commitment. Jesus told the rich young man that in order to gain eternal life he would have to be prepared to give up everything that he had. Unfortunately, he could not do it. 'It is easier for a camel to go through the eye of a needle than for a rich man to enter the kingdom of God' (Mt 19:24). The issue was not money, but rather that God is calling people to come to him with 100% commitment.

Finally, but by no means least, we must receive the free gift that God has given us, receiving forgiveness for the things that we have done and healing from the wounds of the past so that we can have a brand new start and the sure hope of eternal life. God has given us his Holy Spirit as the mark or seal of all that we have inherited and will inherit through Jesus (Eph 1:13).

Gifts

God is a supernatural being with the power to perform mighty miracles. The Holy Spirit is not a spirit being in the sense that New Agers would understand, and not an impersonal force, but rather he is God, part of the Trinity—Father, Son and Holy Spirit. When Jesus ascended into heaven, he promised the disciples that when he was gone, God would come to be with them and all believers. He would come as the Holy Spirit, and he would empower them to live their lives in good relationship with God, enabling them to reach the rest of the world with the good news (Acts 1:7–9).

Being filled with the Holy Spirit, not just once but on a continual basis, should be the natural experience of every Christian. It is not just an added extra (Eph 5:18). Christians really are a people of power: power given to us by God that results in supernatural gifts of the Holy Spirit. You can read more about *these* gifts in the Bible, but we will whet your appetite with this:

> Now about spiritual gifts, brothers, I do not want you to be ignorant. You know that when you were pagans, somehow or other you were influenced and led astray to dumb idols. Therefore I tell you that no-one who is speaking by the Spirit of God says, 'Jesus be cursed,' and no-one can say, 'Jesus is Lord,' except by the Holy Spirit.
>
> There are different kinds of gifts, but the same Spirit. There are different kinds of service, but the same Lord. There are different kinds of working, but the same God works all of them in all men.
>
> Now to each one the manifestation of the Spirit is given for the common good. To one there is given through the Spirit the message of wisdom, to another the message of knowledge by means of the same Spirit, to another faith by the same Spirit, to another gifts of healing by that one Spirit, to another miraculous powers, to another prophecy, to another distinguishing between spirits, to another speaking in different kinds of tongues, and to still another the interpretation of tongues. All these are the work of the one and the same Spirit, and he gives them to each one, just as he determines (1 Cor 12:1–11).

In the light of all the counterfeit supernatural gifts offered by the New Ager and the occultist, it is important for the Christian to understand the gifts of the Holy Spirit and to be able to use them for God's glory. These gifts will build up the church, strengthen you personally, as well as inspiring other people to faith in Christ. Christianity, far from being the spiritual vacuum that many people expect, offers to everyone a life of dynamic supernatural excitement as Christians give themselves to God in humility and openness.

When we look at the New Age in the light of the truth of the Christian gospel, it's clear that the two just don't mix. Little wonder then that many New Agers are vehemently anti-Christian, blaming Christians for the blockage to spiritual growth and cosmic harmony. While the New Age looks towards the dawning of a spiritual awakening of mankind to the mythical energy force they call the one, Christians live in relationship with the one true God as his kingdom steadily advances. For the Christian, the road to personal transformation and global recovery begins with every individual who stands up and says, 'I want nothing to stand between me and God any more.'

A few months ago in our church we baptised an eighteen-year-old lad who had been heavily involved in occult practices and drugs for most of his teenage years. Before he was fully immersed as a tangible sign, both physical and spiritual, of his commitment to Jesus, he said these words, 'I've finally realised that there is only one way to go, and that is to accept God on his terms and not on mine.'

The choice is yours. Will you do the same?

9

Where Do We Go from Here?

Walking down the high street of Chichester, Andrea and a friend noticed that yet another New Age shop had opened up. On investigating inside, Andrea discovered much the same as she'd seen up and down the country as she'd researched the spread of these spiritual phenomena: the same predictable mix of occult paraphernalia, hundreds of crystals and pyramids, runes and tarot cards, pendulums and potions.

It has been interesting to note how quickly and easily these shops have been integrated into the high street mix, and how standard the merchandise that they sell has become.

In the back of the shop there is a comprehensive section of New Age music: a mix of strange atmospheric sounds with a pulsating repetitive beat. Unlike other forms of music, it is a compliment, not an insult, to find yourself yawning halfway through it. The idea is that this mixture of ethereal synthesised sounds—such as the sea lapping against the shore, along with sampled dolphin calls and bird noises—will help you to slow down biorhythmically (in other words, relax) and encourage attunement to the one or to the inner self. There are New Age music tapes for all uses. Some are marketed for specific purposes such as 'cures' for varieties of complaints from insomnia to nervous tension, and some are purely to be used for enhancing meditation techniques.

Also, inevitably, there are hundreds of books available to help individuals understand more of the supernatural world, by exploring their hidden potential, learning to employ some ancient technique of divination, or being put in touch with one of the many spirit guides waiting to be contacted.

So where do we go from here? Interest in the New Age and all things spiritual is ever on the increase. More and more people are actively involved in some of its techniques and practices and are giving their allegiance to the ideas and philosophies of the New Age. We have already seen that the New Age is an enormous subject—such a diverse integration of ideas and practices with little real uniformity that it can seem daunting to approach.

We hope that this book has gone some way towards giving you an idea of the New Age in all its different guises, though we do of course realise that we have been limited, by space, from going into more depth. What we would like to do is leave those of you who are Christians an idea of how you can practically get involved in the New Age head-on, taking time to talk to those who are being carried along on the wave of the New Age scene, in a relevant and sensitive way. Jesus gave us a commission to go to all nations, all people groups, to explain the good news about him in such a way that they will understand and be brought into the experience of an active, ongoing Christian faith (Mt 28:16–20). It is for this reason that we must be prepared to answer the questions that these people are asking about life, God and the planet without being intimidated or ill equipped.

How far do we go?

Generally, there are three attitudes to the New Age that Christians are guilty of. One is the knee-jerk reaction of those who are completely spooked by the whole thing. They feel that because it is clearly not 'Christian', they must steer clear of it in such a way that they would rather cross the road than walk past a New Age shop. They would prefer to run a mile rather than have to face a conversation with someone with a New Age worldview. Too many Christians are so fearful, almost to the point of paranoia, that they are crippled from reaching the very people that we are called to give the good news to.

Clearly, this is not the way to react. To be in such fear of the New Age and all that it entails is not the way that God would want us to live, and it is certainly not the way that Jesus or the disciples of the early church would have dealt with the subject.

As Christians, we need to be certain of where we stand as part of God's kingdom. We have been given a mandate to go to all people, no matter what they might be into. God wants to reach everyone. His mandate to us is not optional; it is the responsibility of every Christian to be an example of what it is to have a real relationship with God, in the things that we say and in the way we live our lives.

The Bible is clear that the kingdom of God and the kingdom of Satan are in conflict and that as Christians we face a battle. 'For our struggle is not against flesh and blood, but against the rulers, against the authori-

ties, against the powers of this dark world and against
the spiritual forces of evil in the heavenly realms' (Eph
6:12). Thankfully, though, God has given us authority
in the name of Jesus to be able to stand against the
enemy, and spiritual armour in order that we can be
prepared to face him.

Another way Christians can react is to go to the
opposite extreme: so blasé about the New Age and
about the increase of occult practices in our schools
and our workplaces that they totally overlook the
dangers of it and find themselves compromising their
faith, as well as incorporating New Age thinking and
techniques into their everyday lives.

The third attitude Christians can take is to decide
unwisely that they can take the New Age on single-
handed, and they end up boldly going where no one
in their right mind would go without an army of
support. Clearly, we need to be wise in making sure
that at all times we are operating from a position of
faith in Jesus, ensuring that we have the full support
and prayer backing of the rest of the church. Too
many lone wolves get picked off as easy targets by the
enemy, ending up hurt, disillusioned and confused as
to what they really believe.

We need to find safe ground! Therefore, we have
put together a few 'hot tips' that we hope will go some
way towards helping us bridge the worldview gap and
enable us to be effective in bringing God's kingdom
to the New Age.

Hot tips for reaching New Agers!

1. Don't be intimidated

We've already said it, but it's very easy to feel
inadequate, particularly since the New Age is such a

huge and diverse subject. The thing that is very important to remember is that people are just people. They may have different ideas and they may dress differently to you, but it doesn't mean that underneath they are not just the same as everybody else. Some people you will feel at ease with very quickly, and some may take a little more time, but as long as you are polite and friendly, people will soon warm to you. At the end of the day, remember this: if it wasn't for the fact that someone had the courage to tell you about Jesus, you wouldn't be a Christian today. Also, God has promised to equip you with everything you will need, and he always keeps his promises.

People who believe something very strongly are often very bold and confident in the delivery of their 'truth'. Don't let this put you off. No matter how eloquent they are and no matter how confidently they can wax lyrical about their spiritual experiences and their personal revelations, they, unfortunately, are deceived.

Remember, you may not know all the answers, but no one is expecting you to be a genius. As long as you are honest and answer the questions that you do know, you'll get along fine. There is nothing to be gained by pretending to know something that you don't, and people are more likely to respect you for being able to say, 'I'm not so sure about that point, but I'll find out for you and let you know as soon as I can.'

2. Don't assume anything

All of us have been guilty at one time or another of judging people because of the way they look or the way they talk. Our preconceived ideas are often very wrong, and we can end up tarring someone with the wrong brush. The Holy Spirit does equip us with the ability to distinguish between spirits so that we will be able to know what, spiritually, is going on in a person's life. However, our advice would be never to assume anything.

We have two ears and only one mouth. Therefore, as the saying goes, we should listen twice as much as we speak. It is important when talking to someone with a New Age agenda that we really listen to what they are saying and what they really think. So often we miss what the real issues are in people's lives because we have made assumptions. The New Age girl in the wheelchair may be content with the fact that she cannot walk, but what she really wants to know is whether it is possible to contact her dead father.

3. Ask questions to reveal

Conversation is a two-way art. There is nothing worse than the situation where one person is doing all the talking while the other stands there shuffling from foot to foot. There is one way of making sure that even the most non-communicative person answers more than a monosyllabic grunt, and that is to ask questions to reveal.

Never ask a question that only requires a 'yes/no' answer, because that is all you will get. Instead, ask questions that encourage people to explain what they think. 'How would you describe God?' 'Why do you think people are born?' They help you to get into conversations quickly, and once people have given you descriptions of what they think, you'll have a better idea of what they are in to.

The more you can find out about where people

are coming from in their thinking, the easier you will find it to communicate the gospel in a way that is relevant to them.

4. Define terms

Sitting in the pub chatting to a guy who seemed to be using a lot of 'Christian' jargon and phraseology, Andrea's sister Samie would have been forgiven for thinking that he *was* a Christian. But using the same words doesn't necessarily imply that you have the same belief. Many New Agers use terms that we as Christians would recognise and use ourselves, but their meanings are completely different. Once again, it's important never to assume anything. Thankfully, Samie didn't, and it turned out that the guy was a member of a New Age group called Eckanker, was actively involved in many occult practices and communicated with his very own spirit guide. His worldview was far removed from that of the Bible.

5. Don't use jargon

It is very easy to get into the habit of using jargon and shortcuts to language in order to explain things, but this is very exclusive. There is nothing worse than trying to talk to someone who is constantly dropping in buzz words and trite phrases which may mean a lot to the 'in' crowd, but actually leave people feeling confused and totally left out.

You may come away from a conversation patting yourself on the back for the full and exhaustive explanation of the gospel that you have given, only to discover that while what you said was very laudable and theologically sound, your listener is really none the wiser. You might as well have been speaking in Swahili for all that they understood.

One friend of ours has a particular habit of bypassing real conversation by using jargon phrases and emphatic hand gestures which are very amusing to the initiated but quite meaningless otherwise. In one five-minute conversation with him, he had enthusiastically expounded that he was, 'Going for it, dovetailing the on-the-ground networking structures with the ongoing framework of teaming it in the translocal context, while taking on board the import-ance of running with the vision for good-newsing the locality, while churching it at the end of the day.' Gobbledegook!

Particularly when explaining the gospel to people, it is essential to make sure that you are as clear and easy to understand as possible. It's far too important a subject to let people go away with 'the wrong end of the stick'.

6. Be prepared

No soldier would go into a battle situation without being prepared for the fight—helmet firmly attached, physically fit, trained and equipped. It should be no different for us.

The apostle Paul wrote to the church in Ephesus that they should put on God's spiritual armour in order to face the battle of opposition to the truth. We need to do the same.

The New Age is very deceptive, and the arguments of many New Agers are very convincing. For this reason we need to be well prepared before we embark on reaching New Agers. This will take a personal commitment to studying the Bible, being sure of what it really says and how it challenges the New Age worldview, and being sure of your own salvation, with 'the helmet of salvation' firmly on your head so that you don't find yourself being swept along with the tidal wave of New Age ideas.

We need to be prepared in prayer, praying for God to intervene in situations, convicting individuals by his Holy Spirit of the truth and giving you more of the Holy Spirit so that you will be more effective. Prayer is essential in bringing us into a closer relationship with God. After all, how many real friendships survive if the two parties never speak to each other? The closer we are to God in prayer, the more clearly we will be able to hear from him how he feels about individuals and their situations, and we will be able to be competent in bringing God's relevant 'now' word to them.

Also, we need to understand the basics of what the New Age is about. Hopefully, this book will have gone some way towards that. As Peter said, we should be prepared at all times and in all situations to give a reason and explanation for our faith (1 Pet 3:15).

7. Don't preach

In conversation with someone who has a New Age worldview, it is wise to be gentle and not to preach at them. People do not respond very well to the truth being rammed down their throats. The moment you start preaching at them, they will switch off and go back inside their shell as effectively as if they were tortoises.

New Agers are used to discussing spiritual matters, to swapping ideas and experiences. They generally have very set ideas and opinions that have been formed as a result of the books they have read, seminars they have attended, or their own life experiences. The best way to endear them to you as a person is to be genuinely interested in what they have to say. After all, these are real people and their opinions are very important to them. The exercise of sharing the gospel message with a person is not a question of who can get the most words in or who can maintain the greatest volume. Far more can be achieved by discussing the differences between the two worldviews, questioning what they believe and asking them as individuals to explain how they would come to terms with the claims of and evidence for Jesus Christ. The best way to bring people to an understanding of the truth is to encourage them to see it for themselves.

The gospel does need to be preached openly. It needs to be preached in such a way that people are able to respond to the truth. However, in one-to-one situations we need to beware of overpowering the conversation and forcing people to agree with what we are saying, either as a way of getting rid of us or because they feel uncomfortable saying no. God wants people to come to him having made a free whole-hearted decision to do so.

It is difficult for people to accept that what they have understood as true is not the truth. The nature of deception is that you don't know you are deceived. It's a bitter pill for people to swallow when told, by what outwardly appears to be an 'arrogant' Christian, that, 'However sincere you are in your belief, you are sincerely wrong.' We need, therefore, to be sensitive in our approach, without losing any of the impact of what we are saying.

There is no point in us feeling guilty that we are spoiling their deception, and watering down our message because we are too afraid of hurting anyone's feelings! We need to be as gracious and sensitive with people, while bringing them to understand the reality of the truth, as Jesus himself would be.

8. Break through the relativity barrier

We have already established that New Agers don't believe in one absolute truth. Their worldview is all inclusive, and they believe that this enables them to be tolerant of everyone's individual beliefs and ideas. In effect, this is not the case. They tend to be very intolerant of Christianity because it challenges their thinking by asserting one absolute truth.

Challenging relative thinking can be very frustrating, because in practice you can talk to someone for a long time, confidently and sincerely putting your case to them, and at the end of it they will smile benignly, pleased that you have your truth and they have theirs. All you have succeeded in doing is letting them know your point of view, but their mind-set gives them the opt-out clause that no matter what you have said or what you believe, it doesn't affect their thinking one iota.

Overcoming this relativity barrier is vital. The way in which you do it we will leave up to you. It is essential that you find ways that suit your own personality and style rather than us giving you a script to learn off pat. In previous chapters we have looked at the paradox of relative thinking: 'How can you be absolutely sure that there are no absolutes?', etc. In the end, the relativity question is a matter of logic.

9. Don't get into swapping 'spiritual' experiences

People do need to know that God is supernatural. He is almighty and all-powerful. We have a God of the impossible who is capable of intervening in our lives in dynamic ways. However, many people with a New Age agenda have had experiences of the supernatural. They may have experienced the counterfeit spiritual power of many New Age and occult practices, and so they have no problem in accepting that there is a spiritual or supernatural realm.

We would advise that you beware of conversations that rely on swapping spiritual experiences. We don't want to get into a situation where we find ourselves trying to match them point for point. Far better is to get to the root issue, which is Jesus, and not get side-tracked by tales of incredible happenings.

10. Answer the questions they are asking

We need to be answering the questions that people are actually asking of us, otherwise we can end up blinding them with science and being totally irrelevant. It's not enough to give your standard three point gospel sermon if the person really wants to know why, if God is a God of love, there is so much suffering in the world.

So it's a matter of listening to what the person is asking and answering in a clear and precise way, without waffling or getting side-tracked into other issues.

Finally, and perhaps one of the most important things of all to remember, is that New Agers are generally very nice, well-meaning people. The majority have come to accept New Age thinking as a result of a deep concern for the state of the planet and of people's lives, and they are genuinely interested in making the world a better place for us all to live in. Many New Agers could teach some Christians lessons in social concern and in caring for others.

Above all, as we face the challenge that the New Age presents, our plea is, be normal! We would like to see all Christians strengthened in their faith and equipped to deal with all that this growing phenomenon presents to us, but without going over the edge.

If we can keep our sense of humour while still recognising the seriousness of the issue, then we will go some way to retaining our sanity. Let's not kiss our brains goodbye, declaring all things New Age. Instead, let us keep our spiritual eyes open to what is going on, being wise in our reactions. Ensuring that we are under the lordship of Jesus Christ, with a strong faith in his power, let's demonstrate by who we are that it is possible to have a relationship with a supernatural God, living in the good of his supernatural kingdom, and still be very natural. As we do this, people will come to recognise the powerful truth of the gospel of Jesus Christ: his power, victory and authority revealed through ordinary, down-to-earth people with whom they can identify.

So much in the world is changing. The New Age is on the increase, and more and more people are searching for answers to their questions. Let it be Christians who are at the forefront of discussions over what is wrong with the world. Let there be Christians who stand up for better education, better health care, and a cleaner, safer environment. Let it be Christians who fight for freedom for the oppressed, for justice and for peace.

Let it be Christians, answering the questions that people are asking, who are heralding in a new age. An age where people are more spiritually minded. An age where people are actively in relationship with God. The age of God's kingdom. An age that will never end.

Notes

1. Virginia Kay Miller, quoted in Marilyn Ferguson, *The Aquarian Conspiracy: Personal and Social Transformation in the 1980s* (Paladin: London, 1982).
2. C. S. Lewis, quoted in Walter Martin, *The New Age Cult* (Bethany House: Minnesota, USA, 1989).
3. Madame Blavatsky, quoted in Bob Larson, *Larson's Book of New Cults* (Tyndale House: Illinois, USA, 1982).
4. Marilyn Ferguson, *op cit.*
5. Shirley MacLaine, quoted in Russell Chandler, *Understanding the New Age* (Word: Milton Keynes, 1989).
6. Z. Budapest, quoted in Douglas R. Groothuis, *Unmasking the New Age* (InterVarsity Press: Illinois, USA, 1986).
7. Nicola Beechs-Squirrel, quoted in David Burnett, *Clash of Worlds* (MARC: Tunbridge Wells, 1990).
8. 'Starhawk', *The Spiral Dance: A Rebirth of the Ancient Religion of the Great Goddess* (Harper & Row: London, 1990).
9. Charles Strohmer, *What Your Horoscope Doesn't Tell You* (Tyndale House: Illinois, USA, 1988).
10. Donald Keys, *Earth at Omega: Passage to Planetization* (Findhorn: Morayshire, 1984).
11. Marilyn Ferguson, *op cit.*
12. Verbal quote from Gerald Coates.

Close Encounters With The New Age

by Kevin Logan

Green issues...meditation techniques...occult journeys into inner space...crystal healing and crystal gazing...new and alternative lifestyles. The New Age appeals to young and old, to those in business and the unemployed—and to many who are simply concerned for the fate of planet Earth.

Vicar and author-journalist Kevin Logan travelled to the very heart of the New Age—Findhorn in Scotland—to meet the people and exchange ideas. His observations will help all those wishing to acknowledge positive aspects of New Age belief and practice, while at the same time highlighting areas of serious concern.

'Fair in its presentation, without compromising Christian beliefs or misrepresenting those of New Agers.'
—STAN STANFIELD
Member, Education Branch
Findhorn Foundation

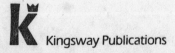

Kingsway Publications